Thinking Through Questions

A Concise Invitation to Critical,
Expansive, and Philosophical Inquiry

Thinking Through Questions

A Concise Invitation to Critical,
Expansive, and Philosophical Inquiry

Anthony Weston

Stephen Bloch-Schulman

Hackett Publishing Company, Inc.
Indianapolis/Cambridge

23 22 21 20   1 2 3 4 5 6 7

For further information, please address
        Hackett Publishing Company, Inc.
        P.O. Box 44937
        Indianapolis, Indiana 46244-0937

        www.hackettpublishing.com

Cover design by Deborah Wilkes
Interior design by Laura Clark
Composition by Aptara, Inc.

Library of Congress Control Number: 2019952425

ISBN-13: 978-1-62466-866-1 (cloth)
ISBN-13: 978-1-62466-858-6 (pbk.)

The paper used in this publication meets the minimum requirements of
American National Standard for Information Sciences—Permanence of
Paper for Printed Library Materials, ANSI Z39.48–1984.

∞

This book is dedicated to our parents, our partners, and our children—to those who raised us to ask good questions and those who keep us always (!) on our toes with more.

Contents

Preface

This book offers an energetic and concise practical guide to the use of questions. Its aim is to help you sharpen your critical questioning, ramp up your creative questioning, and better understand philosophical questioning. It should also leave you more alert to certain common misuses of questioning, so that you are able to turn questionable questions to better effect. In the end, the hope is to help you ask *better* questions: in school, at work, in public forums . . . in life!

Today popular bookstores offer whole books full of questions. One even offers a thousand and one questions "for any occasion." *Thinking Through Questions* offers a few hundred interesting and provocative questions too, if you add them all up—each chapter has extensive exercises—and you could read it just for them. Still, you'll quickly see that better questioning takes much more than amusing yourself or provoking your friends with long lists of questions, even very good ones.

This book aims to teach questioning as an *art*. Better questioning calls upon specific skills, built up through practice and grounded in fuller understanding of questions themselves. You need specific and focused skill to be able to critically question some assertion or argument rather than just accept or reject it. You need other kinds of skills to question your way toward a more expansive range of options when some problem, big or small, seems thoroughly stuck. You need different skills yet again to come to grips with real philosophical questions.

Questioning also may sometimes go awry. It pays to know how to respond to hostile questions or limiting questions. Students also need to know how to better use questions in their studies. This book offers you some first steps in all of these directions. This is why its title has a double meaning: this book offers you ways to use questions to think better, more deeply, more perceptively (that is, to think *using* questions) but also tunes you to some of the ways we ought to question certain questions and be suspicious of them (that is, think critically about the questions themselves).

Chapter 1, **Questions about Questions,** addresses some essential questions about questions themselves. What *is* a question, after all? Why are there so many of them? And why study them anyway?

Chapter 2 outlines **First Steps with Questions**. A first step is to clarify the intention of the question—to consider what kind of response is needed. Next, it is often essential to clarify the question's terms. Then, catch your breath—don't necessarily rush to answer. Entertain more than one answer. Persist when needed . . . which may be often. Also, questioning is not necessarily for the faint of heart: sometimes it takes real courage.

Chapters 3, 4, and 5 consider key questions in each of three areas. Chapter 3 explores **Key Critical Questions**. Critical questioning seeks out the best sources for beliefs or claims and aims to make the best inferences from well-founded facts or experiences. This chapter can stand alone as a rough outline of critical thinking generally, and it can serve equally well as an introduction to a deeper-diving course in critical thinking that begins by giving critical questioning itself a broad context and an approachable rationale.

We're often urged to "think outside of the box," but we're seldom taught *how* to do so. Chapter 4 therefore introduces **Key Expansive Questions**: specific questions that prompt us to think more creatively, for example about problems that may seem thoroughly stuck, and to find new directions and new ideas across the board, even when we may think the possibilities have been exhausted. Creative questioning is a learnable skill—don't ever say, "You can't learn creativity"—but, like other skills, it takes specific methods, and those methods take practice. Once again, this book will get you started, and it will offer some hows and whys for some surprising, and surprisingly powerful, methods of creative and expansive questioning.

Chapter 5 introduces **Key Philosophical Questions**, for example about the assumptions behind our usual beliefs and values and about the ways in which they might be ultimately justified (that is, backed up with decent evidence) . . . or not. Once again our goal is certainly not to "cover" all of philosophy, or even introduce a few major figures, but to orient readers toward philosophical questioning as a way of thinking.

These are skills that philosophers hone over years of practice. Other books—textbooks or original sources—will take you farther in philosophy and in philosophical questioning, just as they can take you farther in critical thinking or creative problem solving. But first you must know what you are getting into, and why. That's enough for this book.

Chapter 6 surveys **Questionable Questions**. These are the problematic questions, including loaded questions, power plays, and other manipulative or fruitless questions and styles of questioning. Chapter 6 offers multiple strategies for reframing and reversing such questionable questions. This too takes skill and practice. You will pick up some methods of fighting back too—constructively, clearheadedly, and even with good humor.

Finally, Chapter 7 is specifically **For Students** at the college or advanced high school level. We distinguish two broadly different types of classes: *Question-Answering Classes* and *Questioning-Centered Classes*. Thinking through questions is necessary in both kinds of classes, but in quite different ways. You need to know the difference, and how to approach each. Come with us—long-time college teachers ourselves—for a quick tour.

As this book took shape, we were grateful for the advice and support of many colleagues, especially Nim Batchelor, Ann Cahill, and Ryan Johnson of the Philosophy Department at Elon, as well as co-conspirators farther afield, especially Rebecca Scott, David Concepción, and Donna Engelmann, who served as a reviewer for Hackett Publishing Company along with a number of other very helpful anonymous readers. Stephen specifically wishes to thank the Critical Whiteness Studies class he and Libby Coyner co-taught (with the help of Nate Jones) in the Spring of 2019. Jonathan Shaw compiled the list of student questions that became part B of the exercise set at the end of the book.

At Hackett, Deborah Wilkes's perceptive and steadfast support for this project were essential from the start, alongside Liz Wilson's and Laura Clark's able management of the production process and deft and circumspect copyediting by Leslie Connor. Many thanks to you all!

Speaking of your authors, meanwhile, you can find more about us in the very last section of this book, should you wish to know why you might want to listen to us (a good question), along with brief accounts of our own favorite kinds of questioning. For now, though, the focus is on *you*. We sincerely hope that this book leaves you a better questioner, even more than a better answerer. Use it well!

aw/sbs
Elon, NC
weston@elon.edu
sschulman@elon.edu

1

Questions about Questions

It's notorious—and wonderful—that young children ask *Why?* about absolutely everything. Maybe as adults we might have more answers than we once did, but even adults actually need lots of questions: *Why? How? When? Really? Who says?* and all the rest. Sometimes we may be trying to find out something we need to know. Other times we may just be amusing ourselves or others. Many other times we are probing, challenging, exploring, seeking out unexpected possibilities, even pleading or lamenting.

We may not think of it this way, but questioning is actually an *art*—a set of abilities we can develop by attention and practice. Questioning is not necessarily a skill that most people have by nature, like walking. It is more like dancing, or auto repair, or child-raising: it's a skill that we can always get better at. In fact, we can get a lot better at it than we imagine at first.[1] If you're lucky, perhaps you know some people who are exceptionally sharp, effective, clearheaded, creative, perceptive questioners. They got that way by doing a lot of questioning and reflecting on it regularly. Which means that *you* can improve your questioning through these practices too.

What Is a Question?

It is easy to list examples of questions. *Will it rain tomorrow? Does she love me? Isn't there a faster way to get to Milwaukee?* One study of young children's questions turned up such gems as *Why do we have eyebrows? Why are you opening that window?* and even—unprompted—the classic *Why did the chicken cross the road?*[2]

---

1. Actually, even walking can be dramatically improved by practice. See Jessica Dweck, "Head Case," *Slate*, August 27, 2010, https://slate.com/news-and-politics/2010/08/the-art-and-science-of-carrying-things-on-your-head.html.

2. Frank Lorimer, "A complete record of the 'Whys' of one child, aged four years and eleven months, during four days," *The Growth of Reason: A Study of the Role of Verbal Activity in the Growth of the Structure of the Human Mind* (Abingdon, UK: Kegan Paul, 1929), 124–26.

Is you is or is you ain't? Is there a God? Are vitamins actually good for you? Is this latest breathless piece of internet "news" really true? And what is the big rush about getting to Milwaukee, anyway?

It is not quite so easy to define the term "question" itself—to say what is the essence of a question. It is not just a matter of punctuation. *Will you please pass the salt?* is really a request, for example, not a question, even though it ends with a question mark. Or again, *Who knows?* is rarely an actual question. There is no curiosity in it; it does not expect an answer.

On the other hand, think of the lullaby's line *Tell me why the stars do shine.* It ends with a period, but it usually does the same work as the question *Why do the stars shine?* Genuine questions may even be posed by non-verbal expressions or gestures. Someone just raises an eyebrow, or a dog cocks her head to one side, and there is a question, sometimes more eloquent than words, and regardless of any punctuation. You can consider the cover of this book for another example.

Crucial to determining if something is a question is deciding what it is meant to *do*. If it somehow expresses curiosity, uncertainty, or doubt, and implies the desire for a response, then, we say, it's a question. To be formal about it, we will state this as a definition, and highlight this definition by putting it in a box, so you are more likely to remember it and we can return to it easily when needed.

> **A question is a request to attend to a curiosity, uncertainty, or doubt, and implies the desire for a response.**

Doubts or uncertainties may be expressed in other ways, of course: as simple reports, for instance, like "I don't believe this!" or "The chance of rain is 80 percent." These are not questions, though, in our view, because they are not typically looking for responses—other than, say, bringing an umbrella.

Of course there are many kinds of curiosities and uncertainties. *Do you want some coffee?* voices quite a different kind of curiosity than *Why did this happen to me?* or *Grandpa, why do we have exactly the same wrapping paper as Santa Claus?* Again, though, all questions highlight something that asks to be answered, inquired into, settled, figured out, negotiated, acknowledged. Questions, as such, create opportunities to go a bit further, a kind of openness toward the future. Even if we don't actually expect a response, a genuine question at least wishes for one!

What Is the Use of Questions?

> If questions are the answer, what is the question?
> —Violet Woodsorrel Oxalis

Why do we even have questions in the first place? What are questions *for*?

We Don't Know Everything

Obviously, we often ask questions to find out something we don't know: the weather tomorrow, what our friends are really thinking, the best recipe for cornbread or apple pie, whether there really was a King Arthur or why a marathon is 26.2188 miles long (odd distance, wouldn't you think?)—not to mention bigger scientific or philosophical questions like how life began, or for that matter what life *is*, or what is really behind UFOs, and even What It All Means.

This is one reason that young children are constantly asking *Why?*: they have so very much to learn. The charming thing about questions like *Grandpa, why do we have exactly the same wrapping paper as Santa Claus?* is that we can see children starting to put 2 and 2 together. Of course, this never really stops. Maybe you and I can put 2 + 2 together with no further ado, but (quick!) *What is the square root of 529?* Oh, and *Why do the aliens who allegedly make crop circles have exactly the same logos as us?*

Helpful people stationed at information desks in airports are prepared to answer questions like *What time zone are we in?* or *Where is the taxi stand?* It is no accident that question marks are the sign of information desks. At the same time, though, they would be thoroughly flummoxed if you ask them questions like *Is there life on Mars?* or *What bait should you use to live-trap a raccoon?* (a question Weston recently desperately needed to answer) or even *Why <u>are</u> there time zones?*, though these are questions of information too.

The world vastly exceeds our knowledge. It's not only young children who have so very much to learn. It's all of us. Indeed, there is far more to know than we ever *can* know. (Probably—but can we know *this* either, for sure?) There are many, many things that we don't even know that we don't know. The world exceeds not only our knowledge but also our ignorance. Questions are sometimes no more than flashlights in a vast dark—but at least we have them.

Curiosity

Many jokes and most riddles are questions. *What did the fish say when she bumped her head?* ("Dam!") *What's another word for "thesaurus"?* Or *What creature walks on four legs in the morning, two legs during the day, and three in the evening?*—the classic riddle of the Sphinx. (Well, who do you think?)

Related to riddles and jokes like these are amusing questions that, lightheartedly or more critically, highlight features of our world we may not have thought about. They arouse curiosity. *When atheists go to court, do they have to swear on the Bible?* Or *When it rains, why don't sheep shrink?* How about *If an ambulance is on its way to save someone, and it runs someone over, does it stop to help them?*[3] Actually, there are rules about this sort of thing. Wouldn't you be curious to know what they are?

In another direction, curiosity may turn into wonder. *Is human action really free? Why are there "interstate" highways in Hawaii?* Christopher Uhl and Dana Stuchul imagine an afternoon stroll with young kids:

"What are those things floating up there?"

"Clouds," the kids respond triumphantly.

"Hmm, what's in them?" asks Dad (the alien).

"Water!" comes the response in unison.

"Hmm . . . how did water get way up there? Hey, why are those clouds moving? And wait a minute, how come that cloud over there is changing shape?"[4]

Actually, even scientists are not sure how so much water ended up on Earth. The going theory, believe it or not, is comets—millions of them. More than one question that intrigues kids on a summer afternoon drives cutting-edge scientific inquiry too.

---

3. These questions are from http://www.crazythoughts.com/, accessed April 10, 2019.

4. From Christopher Uhl and Dana Stuchul, *Teaching* as if *Life Matters* (Baltimore: Johns Hopkins University Press, 2011), 52.

Things May Not Be What They Seem

We also need questions because (surprise!) we cannot always trust what we are told or see. *Questioning* can also mean *not entirely trusting*—and there are often very good reasons for doubt.

Plain old lies are no news in our era of "fake news." People are trying to mislead us, big time. And not just politically. Some studies claim that people lie on an average of twice a day (though the lying is not evenly distributed: nearly a quarter of the lies were told by only 1 percent of the sample).[5] Another study suggests that 90 percent of people lie in online dating profiles.[6] Eighty-three percent claim to have read books they haven't read. Some people even make up statistics! For example, we just made up that last one. (Was there any way you could tell? Sounded good, though, didn't it?) And of course, we lie to ourselves too. Sexists or racists may be absolutely convinced that they are not the least prejudiced, but act that way, even flagrantly, nonetheless.

Total misrepresentation is also possible even when no outright lies are told. Camouflage, deception, the carefully constructed public facades of board meetings and Thanksgiving dinners, movie stars or political candidates—what's the *real* story? Questions are our ways of asking, or at least reminding ourselves that we don't really know.

Not asking a few questions can sometimes be lethal. *Hey Trojans, here's a nice big trophy horse to commemorate your victory over us! Haul it right inside your city walls and then give yourselves a really good night's sleep—you've earned it!* A few questions before turning in would have been a good idea.

Appearances can mislead even when no deception is intended. Studies of UFO reports suggest that the vast majority are of totally natural phenomena that are simply mis-seen. Large numbers of people have even called the police to report UFO invasions, when all they were really seeing were bright stars during a power outage at night. Again a few double-checking questions might have saved everyone a

---

5. Gad Saad, "How Often Do People Lie in Their Daily Lives?," *Psychology Today*, November 30, 2011, https://www.psychologytoday.com/blog/homo-consumericus /201111/how-often-do-people-lie-in-their-daily-lives, accessed August 27, 2019.

6. Steve Mirksy, "My Unfunny Valentine," *Scientific American*, February 14, 2007, https://www.scientificamerican.com/podcast/episode/C1597486-E7F2-99DF -310BFD76D5647B1D/, accessed August 27, 2019.

lot of upset and trouble—and made for a lot more wonder too (that is, at the stars).

Much of What Seems "Obvious" Isn't

Some people think that a lot of things are "just obvious." And indeed, some things *are* obvious. Still, arguably, most of what seems obvious probably really isn't. Even when there may be truthful intentions, the truth itself is often layered, hidden, obscure, complicated. Questions are a good way to avoid being too sure about things.

We know that the Earth is round, for instance, but for centuries people were just as confident that it was flat. In fact you can still find quite serious "Flat Earthers" online, even today, complete with elaborate attempts at arguments and evidence. On the other hand, if you think about it, maybe it really *wasn't* so obvious that the Earth is flat. Seafaring people from antiquity could see that ships disappear beneath the horizon when they head out of port. If the Earth were flat, wouldn't ships instead just look smaller and smaller until they disappeared—or vanish all of a sudden (falling off the edge), never to come back? So doesn't the Earth actually "obviously" look *round*?

Hmm . . . so why do we take it for granted that the ancients thought the world was flat? Good question!

Many Things Need Challenging

To question is also in part to challenge. For instance, less noted in the fond stereotypes about young children's question *Why?* is that the same question tends to come back a few years later with a lot more edge. *Why do I have to do my homework? Why can't I use the car? Why do I have to be polite to people that even you don't like?* Though it might not make for family harmony, this kind of questioning is still useful as young people prepare to make their own way in the world. Parents might even welcome it as an occasion to rework the rules in a more cooperative way. (*How?* Another good question—but for another book.)

Meanwhile, one or two things might just possibly also need challenging in the larger world around us—right? Once again the questions may be unsettling, and the answers may take a great deal of work if they are possible at all, but the process may be necessary all the same.

In a classic story, a pretentious emperor struts down the street showing off his fabulous new clothes that everyone, echoing the extremely well-compensated "weavers," says can only be seen by the virtuous. In reality he's stark naked—and, on some unadmitted level, both he and everyone else knows it (ahhh . . . lying to oneself again). Still, everyone plays along—who'd want to declare that they see nothing?—until a child bursts out to ask: *Why is the emperor wearing no clothes?* And then it is all over.

So mightn't there still be naked emperors, so to speak, among us today? Who or what? How can we tell? More good questions . . .

Thinking outside of the Box

Finally, the actual world is very far indeed from fixed or finished. When it comes to future possibilities and alternative actions, the possibilities, as the saying goes, are endless. Questions create a sense of freedom—room to move—that is not present if you simply start with the "givens" and take on the world's seeming burdens with a sigh of resignation. When the world feels fixed and closed, in fact, we *especially* need questions to open it back up: to provoke our thinking "outside of the box." What lies behind or outside of what seems to be given?

Paper or plastic? What else is possible? Bringing your own cloth bag, as many people are now doing? Many stores sell them, or even give them away. Or bringing a backpack? Or eating the food right in the store?

You *have* to get a job right after college, right? Or, do you? What if you travel the world after college, before settling down to a job? Hike the Appalachian Trail? Join the Peace Corps? Start the next world-changing business in your spare time in your garage, like the richest person in today's world?

We *have* to have cars in cities, right? We *have* to raise the dikes in New Orleans and elsewhere to defend against rising waters and stronger storms, right? Or, do we? Do we really "have no choice"? In cities on the edge of rising waters, like New Orleans, *must* we just raise the dikes and hope they'll hold next time? What about moving the most flood-prone neighborhoods instead? What about building them on stilts . . . or pontoons?

Why Study Questions?

Why should we *study* questions? That's a great question—glad you asked.

Appreciation

Our first answer is simple: for sheer appreciation. We've suggested that questions are useful, powerful, often necessary . . . but you are also already catching a hint, we imagine, that in our view questions are also intriguing and just plain satisfying. Questions are often a lot of fun.

Not even young children's endless *Why?* questions are merely some sort of nuisance. They're not just "cute" either. Young children's questions are lovely manifestations of the awakening of young minds in a world of wonder, where everything is new and puzzling and fascinating. Questioning—even impatiently, sometimes with the next question tumbling before the last one is answered, and even when they have a teenage edge—is what young minds *do*, and *should* do. (And yes, we have had children ourselves. We've also *been* children ourselves . . . you too, we somehow suspect.)

We may not have all the answers. So what? Maybe adults are too invested in having answers. Indeed, we think that the association of questions with children is actually rather suggestive. There can be a great joy in questions too: in probing and wondering, as well as talking to all manner of people, or reading around on Wikipedia or wherever your questioning may take you. Questioning can be one small way of reclaiming some of that youthful delight in openness.

Building Skill

So we are pleased to celebrate questions for their own sakes. After that, though, we buckle down to *study* questioning for a thoroughly practical general reason: because asking better questions allows us to think and live better.

Of course, again, anyone can put a question mark at the end of a sentence and make a question out of it. Most people can also kick a soccer ball around a field too, but that doesn't make them a soccer player, let alone the next Mia Hamm. As we said at the start, skill at any such thing takes practice. And you practice questioning by, well, questioning and thinking about questioning.

Expansive thinking, for instance, uses distinctive kinds of questions to prompt or even force more open-ended and unusual associations. You have to know what they are and understand why they are necessary, and then get used to using them. Critical thinking builds upon its own set of quite sharp questions—not always familiar (in fact they are far from familiar, judging from a lot of public discourse today) and needing practice too. Philosophers use yet other kinds of questions to help us clarify assumptions, key ideas, and basic principles. You can always get better.

Sometimes questioning is personally challenging as well. We may have to reconsider long-held or cherished beliefs, and hold ourselves and others to account. This can take a great deal of interpersonal skill, and sometimes a good bit of courage as well. And then there are the "obvious" things that, as the detective Sherlock Holmes memorably put it, are actually not even true. Again, learning to question all of these, productively and effectively, takes time and work.

Targeting Curiosity

Sometimes we can stoke our curiosity just by asking factual questions of each other or online. *What is the origin of corn? Can blind people see in their sleep? Who is DJ Casper and is there a Cha Cha Slide Part 1?*[7] Usually, though, it takes *methods* that we must learn—another reason to study questions ever more closely.

For example, we can learn from scientists to pose research questions that are specifically and usefully answerable using scientific methods. We can learn from philosophers to use hypothetical questions to focus our thinking about the implications of certain principles or concepts. And sometimes these seemingly hypothetical questions become all too relevant, like this one: *What should an autonomous vehicle do if faced with an imminent and unavoidable deadly accident? Allow the person in the car to be killed, or a passer-by?* This used to be just hypothetical, like science fiction, but now carmakers really need to know. Trying out various answers may give us a provocative

---

7. A hat tip to the podcast *Every Little Thing* for these questions. See https://gimletmedia.com/shows/every-little-thing/dvheek for all sorts of interesting answers to these profound questions.

and otherwise unavailable perspective on what we usually take for granted—and raise questions about our true ethical values as well.

Good Citizenship

Again, it's no news that we are awash in baseless claims, misinformation, and "fake news." Google the question *Is climate change real?*, for example, and a mere 664 million "answers" instantly come up (as of July 2019). Really? What's more, the top hits (along with literally tens of millions of others) are typically climate-change denial sites, paid for (someone has very big money in this—good questions would be *Who?* and *Why?*) and carefully engineered to come up at the top of search engines' queues—which does *not* mean that they are in any way the most reliable or well-founded. Quite the contrary . . . but how many people look beyond the first page of hits?

Constantly subjected to such claims, we need to learn to pose focused and specific kinds of questions and to question (indeed often just to *search*) more deeply. This kind of skill with questions is in fact a vital form of intelligent citizenship, especially in today's supercharged public debates.

Likewise, asking good questions within and about science requires a focus on actual evidence and how that evidence was gathered, as well as some sense for baseline plausibility and an appreciation of how science operates. It's no objection to a scientific claim or theory, for example, that it is continuously being tested as it goes (as in "it's just a theory"). On the contrary, continuously being questioned, and sometimes re-formed as a result, is what makes scientific theories *strong*. Few other kinds of supposed knowledge are so thoroughly and constantly questioned.

Asking good questions about economic, social, or political arrangements takes a sense of their historical origins along with the freedom of mind to imagine alternatives. *Why are there only two main political parties in the United States? What was the world like before racism? What if the best things in life really are free?* Explicitly or implicitly, questions like these not only challenge certain specific things but also challenge the idea that things in general must be more or less the way they are. No: the suggestion instead is that things are the way they are for certain very specific reasons—sometimes bad ones—and that they can also be changed. Questioning them is the beginning.

Freeing the Mind

When Einstein famously declared that "imagination is more important than knowledge," he didn't mean "imagination" in the sense of
undirected daydreaming. He meant a certain kind of rigorous and
focused questioning. One of Einstein's breakthrough "thought experiments" asked, *How would the universe look if we were riding a light
beam?* The cool but strange answer is that (roughly) you would see
nothing at all. Time would stand still.[8] Not that Einstein or anyone
else ever did or could travel so fast, but the mere hypothetical question prompted him to develop the general theory of relativity . . . and
so to turn physics on its head.

Finally, we want to leave you with just a mention of Zen "koans,"
a special type of mind-expanding question (more on koans later in
this book).

> A student one day remarked offhandedly to her Zen teacher that "of
> course, no one can really know what another person is experiencing."
> Her teacher replied: "If no one can really know what another person
> is experiencing, how can you know that I am not experiencing what
> another person is experiencing?"

There's really no answer to this—so it might be best not to look for
one. Confronted with such a question, the best response might be a
hearty laugh, or to go swimming. But might you also, just possibly,
find yourself paying a little better attention to *whoever's* experience
might come along?

Cosmological thought experiments and Zen koans are not for
everyone—at least not all the time. Still, at such "extremes" we can
see something that is not always so evident in everyday forms of
questioning: again, that there is openness and freedom in well-done
questioning. Learning to think better through questions brings with
it a range of mind-broadening and mind-opening shifts: from a more
fixed and closed sense of the world to a more dynamic and open
feeling; from insistence on "sure" answers to curiosity; from a sense of
*im*possibility to a sense of possibility. Questions open the world to us
in new and animating ways. And hurrah for that, we say.

---

8. "As you approach light speed, distances and time intervals become dilated to infin-
ity, everything appears to be infinitely far away and to take an infinitely long time."
From Silas, "The Doctor," https://www.quora.com/If-you-were-riding-on-a-light
-beam-i-e-were-a-massless-observer-magically-traveling-at-the-speed-of-light
-what-would-you-see-around-you, accessed July 19, 2018.

No Questions Allowed!?

Another way to get a perspective on the power and importance of questions is to consider settings in which specific questions are actually *prohibited*. What is the world like without them?

One such setting is societies in which people are so intimidated that they keep their heads down and ask no deeper questions, no matter what happens. They may ask how to accomplish something specific, but they do not dare ask (or maybe even think) questions about who is in charge or why things are the way they are. Some such societies exist in our world right now. If you are reading this book, at least without hiding it under the covers and living in fear, you aren't in one of them. Be grateful—and use that freedom as fully as you can.

We might ask a deeper question (ha!) here too. Why would any society ban these kinds of questions? Cracking down takes a lot of time and energy—why would that be worth it?

One reason is that, paradoxically, those who make and enforce the prohibition quite likely realize that the whole system is profoundly question*able*—so questionable and so vulnerable, in truth, that it could not survive open questioning. More naked emperors. So they cannot *allow* it to be questioned—to face the questions. Likewise, some people cannot allow themselves to question some story that they have lived by, and they therefore try, if they can, to force others around them live by that story too. And usually force is the only way—which is why the consequences are so awful for everyone else. This is also, once again, why the practice of questioning is so very important to practice and defend, and to do well.

FOR PRACTICE

1A

Can you imagine living without any questions? How? Would you want to? Why or why not? Why don't you try it: see if you can avoid asking or even thinking of any questions for, say, two days. Is this hard? Why?

1B

What might you want from a book on questions, anyway? Why are you reading this one?

Don't just say that you were assigned to read it, even if you were. Do you read everything you are assigned? What would make you put this book down—or get mad and throw it across the room? Contrariwise, what would make you reread it five times and buy copies for everyone you know? (We recommend this.)

1C

Most of the following sentences have question marks, but are they actually questions? Why or when? In what contexts are they most likely something else (not questions)?

SAMPLE

Question: How are you?

Sample answer:
"How are you?" is just a way of saying hello, and you are supposed to automatically say "Fine"—if you answer at all. Strangely enough, it is not a real question. We can see this because we know that we'd be surprised if someone stopped and seriously tried to answer, like, "Well, I woke up with a headache, maybe it's the weather, but I feel much better after a cup of coffee, thank you, though I have really been wondering about the Electoral College . . ."

Comment:
This is a strong start, but it only answers part of the question. It is true that "How are you?" often plays out the way this answer suggests. But not always. For example, a close friend who has not seen you in a while might well want a detailed answer. Here it would be a real question. If

your doctor or therapist asks how you are, it's also very likely a serious question. They may not care about what you think about the Electoral College, but they may want specific answers about your shoulder or your mood.

1.   Mirror, mirror, on the wall, who is the fairest one of all?

2.   What would Buddha do?

3.   Hot enough for ya?

4.   Tell me about your mother.

5.   What if time stopped suddenly for five seconds?

6.   Am I my brother's keeper?

7.   Do you take this person to be your lawful wedded spouse?

8.   Who let the cat out of the bag?

9.   Why is the night sky dark?

10. Why do we kill people who kill people in order to show that killing people is wrong?

11. If cats always land on their feet but toast always lands butter-side down, what would happen if you tape a piece of toast to the back of a cat and let 'er drop?

12. Will you shut up?

1D

Here are some recent news headlines. After reading this chapter, what good questions might you ask of them? Share your lists.

SAMPLE

Headline: *Costa Rica Still the Happiest Country in the World, Studies Show*

Sample answer:

I thought of at least four good questions:

#1:   Studies, eh? Who is doing these studies? Might they have a slant?

#2:. How do these studies measure happiness? Happiness seems subjective enough that it is hard to measure objectively, but these studies must have some definite measure if they can numerically rank the happiness of different countries. What is it? Would different measures yield a (possibly very) different ranking?

#3:   So why <u>are</u> the Costa Ricans so happy, anyway? Do they have some secret? What is it?

#4:   Why is this news? Maybe because we (Americans?) think <u>we</u> must be the happiest? (Actually the United States is 105th in this ranking—whoa, how does <u>that</u> happen?)

Comments:

This answer is well done, partly because it questions well below the surface. It asks who is doing these studies, how they measure happiness, and why this and not a million other possible stories are "news"—all good examples of applied curiosity, and a little bit of mistrust too. There's more to find out—and, well, to question.

We also give the writer a lot of credit for doing some additional research (at least to find out that the United States is more or less at the bottom of a ranking that puts Costa Rica on top), which should also help answer the question of what measures these studies used. These likely can be questioned in turn. A still better answer could pursue some of these further questions (see http://time.com/3594543/happiest-countries-maps-costa-rica/).

One important insight here is that good questions often require work. Research is one type of such work. We might be inclined to think that questions emerge from just the act of thought—but the best questions often come after some exploring or research is done and answers are still not forthcoming.

1. *Autonomous Cars May Be Entering the Most Dangerous Phase*

2. *How Banks Could Control Gun Sales If Washington Won't*

3. *When Scientists Study Dreams*

4. *The Average American Sees 5,000 Movies in a Lifetime*

5. *New Report Finds No Evidence That Having Sex with Robots Is Healthy*

6. *Kate Middleton Reportedly Felt Meghan Markle "Used Her to Climb the Royal Ladder" and Told Her So at Christmas*

7. *YBN Almighty Claims He Met Blac Chyna on Christian Mingle*

8. *If Climate Change Wrecks Your City, Can It Sue Exxon?*

9. *Fake News Does Much, Much Better on Twitter than Real News—So We're All Doomed*

10. *Newfound "Organ" Could Be the Biggest in Your Body*

11. *Watching TV Can Kill You*

12. *Over $60 Billion Wiped Off Value of Cryptocurrencies in 24 Hours as Bitcoin Slide Continues*

1E

Do you think the following subjects need questions? (Hint: totally.) What questions? Again, make lists of your questions and share them.

SAMPLE

Subject: Humor

Sample weaker answer:
One question I have is how I can come up with good jokes to entertain my friends. I want to be a funnier person! Also, who's the funniest comedian today? You could also ask if humor is always appropriate. It doesn't seem OK to laugh at someone's car accident or bad grade but when life is boring it's not too funny either.

Sample stronger answer:
What makes something funny? In general, I mean. We laugh at all sorts of things, from puns and silly one-liners to the comedy of Shakespeare and Tina Fey. Is the funniness the same in every case?

This makes me wonder why we laugh in the first place. Do other animals laugh too? What if they're laughing but we can't tell? What if they're laughing at <u>us</u>?

Can anything be funny? American comedians had a hard time right after the 9/11 attacks, but why is it OK to make (some) jokes about it now? (Or is it?) I wonder if humor may be partly a way to come to terms with a world that is sometimes too painful or taboo to look in the face. This could explain why there are so many jokes about death and sex. Only yesterday I was wondering what my parents did to fight boredom before the internet. I asked my seventeen siblings, but they didn't know either.

Comments:
The weaker answer is short and offhand and starts out rather self-centered. Notice, though, that it is not hard to go deeper with its question of "how to be funnier." With some more thinking, it could turn into the question of what makes a joke or anything else funny in the first place—the stronger answer's lead question. (So one moral of this story is: Stick with it. Don't just write down the first questions that occur to you—use your first ones to develop more thoughtful ones.)

Asking whether humor is always appropriate is a good move, but in the weaker answer it's over as soon as it starts. The second answer sticks with the original point and, instead of leaving to go elsewhere, takes the same question several steps further, offering a thoughtful speculation about the nature of some kinds of humor, and even ends with a (somewhat) funny sex joke.

1.   Love

2.   Sex

3.   Life (in the sense of how to live well)

4.   Life (in the sense of the biological phenomenon)

5.   Food

6.   Success

7.   Work

8.   Money

9.   Race

10. Time

11. Space aliens

12. The future

1F

Primo Levi was a Jewish man who was forced to endure a long journey in a cattle car on his way to a concentration camp during World War II. Levi was hungry and very thirsty. Deep into the journey, the train stopped, and, spotting an icicle, Levi reached out to break it off. Before he could bring the icicle to his lips, a hulking guard grabbed his arm and snatched the icicle away. Levi looked at the guard and asked, "Warum?" ("Why [have you done this]?"). The guard responded, "Hier ist kein warum" ("There is no 'why' here"). Reflecting on this incident, Fritz Stern wrote: "This 'Hier ist kein warum' stands against everything that is human and constitutes a form of verbal annihilation."[9]

What do you think Stern means by the phrase "stands against everything that is human"?

---

9. Cited in Uhl and Stuchul, *Teaching* as if *Life Matters*, 65.

2

First Steps with Questions

You may think through questions either by yourself or with others. Others may also pose questions to you, for many different reasons. This chapter offers some first steps toward taking up questioning in more depth, regardless of who is doing the asking.

Clarify Intentions

A question, remember, is a request to attend to a curiosity, uncertainty, or doubt, and implies the desire for a response. A first and very practical step to consider with any question, then, is what is the curiosity, uncertainty, or doubt behind it. This allows us to consider what kind of response is wanted or would be helpful.

> Little Jenny comes home from preschool and asks, "Mommy, where did I come from?" Mommy takes a deep breath and tells her all about when a man and woman love each other very much, and sperm and egg, and penis and vagina. Jenny listens, thinks, and then says: "Oh, that's neat, my friend Charlie says he comes from Chicago."[1]

Obviously, it is a good idea to check to be sure you understand what questioners actually want to know before jumping in to answer their questions—and clarify the questions you ask, both so you understand what you want and can be clear about it to others.

Even the simplest-sounding questions sometimes reflect complex and unclear intentions right below the surface. *Who cares?*, for example, is grammatically a question, of course, but often in practice it is a kind of throwaway assertion, something like "It doesn't matter!"—which may or may not be true. At other times it may be a desperately important question. *Who does care?* Things that may seem

---

1. Related by Lisa Belkin in "When Very Young Children Ask Very Hard Questions," *Huffington Post*, December 12, 2011, updated January 31, 2012, https://www.huffingtonpost.com/2011/12/12/when-very-young-children_n_1143086.html, accessed July 8, 2019.

insignificant to some people may be quite significant to others. (Who cares—about, say, the engineering of cardboard? Well, a lot of people, because without it much of our economy would grind to a halt.) Sometimes *Who cares?* can even be a cry for help—a plea for reassurance that someone actually does care about you.

Likewise, the question *Can I help you?* has several quite different meanings, including *What the hell do you think you're doing?* You wouldn't want to answer the literal question ("Well thanks, officer, how about if you drive the getaway car?") when you are actually being asked something entirely different.

The Star-Spangled Question

Have you ever noticed that the lead stanza of "The Star-Spangled Banner" is almost entirely made up of *questions?*

> Oh, say can you see by the dawn's early light
> What so proudly we hailed at the twilight's last gleaming?
> Whose broad stripes and bright stars through the perilous fight,
> O'er the ramparts we watched were so gallantly streaming?

Technically these lines ask after the flag flying over Fort McHenry during the British bombardment of Baltimore harbor in 1814, and the answers were and are known: the defense held, and the next morning "our flag was still there." The real question, though—the kicker—is the familiar refrain:

> Oh say, does that star-spangled banner yet wave
> O'er the land of the free and the home of the brave?

Francis Scott Key makes the defense of Fort McHenry into an allegory for all Americans to carry freedom and bravery—courage and persistence—forward in the same spirit. Are we still the "land of the free," he asks the future—that is, us. The genius of Key's lyrics is that it is *still* a question, for every generation of Americans.

Given Key's own problematic views about African Americans (he wanted them to go back to Africa), it is striking that during the Civil War era, a new stanza was composed to make the song speak to the freedom of African Americans, explicitly answering Key's question from an abolitionist point of view:

> By the millions unchained, who our birthright have gained,
> We will keep her bright blazon forever unstained!

Likewise, where is special courage and devotion to freedom needed *now*? Is the battle ever really over? Oh, and how many other countries do you think have questions for their national anthem?

Clarify Terms

Another basic move with questions is to ask what their terms mean, concretely and specifically. Even such a simple question as *Will it be nice out today?* depends on what you mean by "nice"—and for that matter on the setting. A nice winter day is quite different than a nice summer day. A nice day in Iceland is not the same as a nice day in Tahiti.

During his 1980 presidential campaign against Jimmy Carter, Ronald Reagan famously posed the question *Are you better off today than you were four years ago?* Despite its use as political rhetoric (the automatic answer was supposed to be *No!*), this question is actually complex. What do we mean by "better off"? By some of the usual measures, things were indeed worse in 1980 than 1976. By other measures, things were better. So what measures are to be used? What do we most care about as a people?

"Diversity"

A group of Bloch-Schulman's students were once working on the question *Why isn't there more diversity on our campus?* He asked them, *What kind of diversity are you asking about? Do you think we need more very tall and very short people? More people with tattoos?*

After all, our campus is sorely lacking in tattoos. Or, more sincerely, *Do we need more types of majors? More economic diversity? More racial diversity?*

The students finally decided that what they meant was *Why aren't there more African Americans and Latinx people on campus?* Then Bloch-Schulman asked what they meant by "on campus." In fact, there are quite diverse populations right here, if we pay attention to all the people who work "on campus." Much of our housekeeping, food service, and groundskeeping staff is African American and Latinx. They are not a small population for our university as a whole, but they are a small portion of those who are visible; many are behind the scenes in kitchens or cleaning at night. They are not, for the most part, those in power—students, faculty, staff, and administrators. Which of course raises more questions . . .

Take Your Time

Some questions may be urgent, like *Where's the fire?* or *¿Dónde está el baño?* Others may call for some simple piece of information, like *What time is it?* though even this could have a range of answers, from "Showtime, showtime" to "6:13" to "Time to call for help." Often, though, we can think further through questions—and sometimes, at least, we should. Don't always rush through to answers, but instead take some time with them, to catch your breath and look around.

Reagan's question *Are you better off today than you were four years ago?*, for example, could have prompted a useful discussion. It might even have been the occasion for a thoughtful discussion about national goals. Again, what measures of "better off" *ought* to be used? And is the question whether I am (personally?) better off even the right question? (Is the *country* better off?) To rush into answering seems like a way of not really thinking. Likewise with Bloch-Schulman's students' question about diversity. Taking more care with it, they ended up with changed perspective on a campus they thought they already knew very well.

Questions That Need Unpacking

Does This Baby Make Me Look Straight? is the title of a recent book by Dan Bucatinsky.[2] It's a catchy and provocative question. If you are going to try to answer such a question, though, you first need to *unpack* it.

We'd say there are at least three questions packed into this one. Two are fairly straightforward: *What is it to "look straight"?* What typical assumptions do we make about gay and straight people? and *Specifically, what stereotypes does carrying a baby evoke?* Does it fit "looking straight"?

Bucatinsky's book gives detailed, poignant, and often hilarious answers to these questions. At bottom, though, he is also posing a third one: *What do we really think about those stereotypes?* Bucatinsky's challenge at its core is to rethink them. However you answer this question, the first step is to recognize it explicitly.

Why does the US National Women's Soccer Team do so well? might be a question comparing the US women's team to women's national soccer teams from other countries. Probably, though, it needs to be unpacked much further. For example, it could instead (or also) be asking why the US women do so much better against the world than the US men do. Or, it might be asking why US women's teams do so well in soccer when they do not necessarily do as well in many other sports. It might even be asking all of these questions at once.

To understand the women's soccer team's success, you'll need some backstory. US schools used to support few or no sports for girls, but after 1972, when Title IX required equal opportunity, soccer became a prime option. In much of the rest of the world, though, especially in many of the most soccer-obsessed countries, soccer still barely exists as an option for women. Nothing at all against US women athletes, then, but it's not a surprise that the US women's team does well against the rest of the world. Of course, we don't know how many teams would have to compete against the US women to displace them from their current dominance; we just know that there aren't that many yet.

---

2. Subtitled *Confessions of a Gay Dad* (New York: Atria Books, 2012).

And the men? Men's soccer is *the* sport in much of the rest of the world, and has been so for much longer than it has even been recognized in the United States. The US National Men's Soccer Team therefore enters a world of stiff and long-established competition, while at the same time US male athletes also have many more options—other and mostly more traditional sports—that draw off many good players. Nothing at all against the US Men's National Soccer Team either, then, but it's no surprise that they have such an uphill battle internationally.

So the answer is not so much about US women athletes per se as about the status of women's versus men's sports generally in the United States and the rest of the world. "It's complicated!"

Entertain More Than One Answer

Questions like *How are you?* or *Is human action really free?* or even *Does that star-spangled banner yet wave o'er the land of the free and the home of the brave?* all can be answered in more than one way, sometimes even opposite ways, depending on who is asking, who is being asked, and how the question is unpacked. The sea shanty that starts out asking *What do you do with a drunken sailor?* follows up with a half dozen different answers. And as you all know, there is a large cottage industry answering the classic *Why did the chicken cross the road?*

Of course other questions have fewer answers, and some have only one, like *What time zone are we in?* (because there is only one time zone for each place) or *What is the ratio of a circle's diameter to its radius?* (Pi!) Still, there are probably fewer questions with only a single answer than we may think. So take care not to close down your answering too soon. When you find one good answer, don't assume there isn't another or even better answer. Maybe there is a still tastier recipe for apple pie, or some other reason your friend is making faces at you, or a way to build even better mousetraps. Keep questioning!

It may seem that at least in mathematics and the natural sciences there can only be one right answer to most questions. But think again! Is 1 + 1 necessarily even 2? It depends on the meaning of terms, for one thing: in base 2 the equation looks quite unexpected, like this: 1 + 1 = 10. And if you add one drop of water to another one drop of water, usually you get *one* somewhat larger drop of water (so, 1 + 1 = 1). Meanwhile, there are competing scientific explanations for many phenomena, and only careful testing over time will allow us to narrow down the best answers. Or maybe some new and better explanations will emerge tomorrow.

Chapter 4 will give you a wide range of tools for expansive thinking. The very first step, though, is to remember that there usually *can* be more than one answer to any question. We certainly won't know, anyway, unless and until we look for them!

"The Barometer Question"

A classic illustration of this point is a delightful story about a barometer that has attained the status of internet meme (so the question of what is the truth behind it may be another question that has more than one answer—but that is not our concern right now).

In the story, a physics student is asked a routine question on an exam: *How can you use a barometer to tell the height of a tall building?* There is a standard, expected answer: measure the air pressure at ground level and at the top of building, and figure the height from the difference, since air pressure decreases with height at a known rate.

But the story goes that this particular student (some say it was Niels Bohr, who later became one of the world's leading physicists) was fed up with his professor's rote style of teaching and insistence that there is just one right answer. So Bohr (or whoever) came up with half a dozen *un*expected but technically correct alternative answers, like throwing the barometer off the roof and calculating the building's height from the time it took to smash to the ground, or counting the number of barometer lengths from bottom to top of the building and then multiplying by the length of the barometer, and (our personal favorite) pawning the barometer and using the proceeds to bribe the building superintendent to tell him the height of the building from the blueprints.

None of these methods were anything like what the professor had in mind (the story sometimes goes that the student was, at least initially, failed), and some are distinctly unfriendly to the barometer, but they are perfectly correct as well as amusing answers to the actual question. (A number of other answers are possible too—why don't you see how many more you can think of yourself?) The moral of the story: inventively multiplying answers is as possible in science as anywhere else.

Persist

"The Emperor's New Clothes" is partly the story of a put-down. Everyone pretends to see the emperor's marvelous new garments, including the strutting naked emperor himself, since no one wants to seem less than virtuous. Only a child asks, *Why is the emperor wearing no clothes?* In some versions of the story, the adults immediately shush the child up, out of fear, hypocrisy, or both. "*Of course* the emperor has wonderful new clothes . . . but we could hardly expect a child to see them, could we?" Or: "What a cute question!" Or: "Shut up, kid!"

It happens all the time. Someone may ask a question only to be patronized or dismissed rather than answered. "Who are you to be asking?" or "Obviously you don't know the first thing about this subject." Or you may just be ignored.

You may respond to this in various ways. Sometimes you may really be powerless to carry the question on—so find some other way to help out, or just *get* out. When you can, though, persist. Sometimes questions may need to be asked repeatedly before they are heard or answered.

Then there are put-*offs*.

Caller: Can you tell me why I have to give you my email address?

Rep: It's company policy.

Fine, but *why* is it "company policy"? If there really is any policy at all, in truth, as opposed to just a standard "put-off" answer. "Company policy," all by itself, is not a reason.

Or again:

Caller: Can you tell me why I have to give you my email address?

Rep: We need your address because it is necessary for our records.

Well, maybe . . . but *why* is it "necessary"?—that was the actual question. Maybe that question actually could be answered. If you are dealing with the sort of product that might have recalls, for example, the producer might need ways to contact buyers. So far, though, the supposed answer is just a re-assertion disguised as an explanation. It's needed because it's needed. Cool. The question is still *Why?* (And to whose benefit?—i.e., what else might your address be used for?) Don't be put off—keep asking.

"Are There Any Questions?"

"Questions don't come very naturally to us," critical thinking professor and author Gerald Nosich declared in a recent podcast. "It takes some work and a good deal of practice to ask questions, and it also takes some familiarity with the kinds of questions that would be beneficial to ask." He goes on:

> So you've seen these movies, usually it's a crime movie about the police, or it's a military movie where the captain is addressing a group of thirty people, and he says: "Okay, we're going to go into this operation and your group are going to go into this from the left, and you're going to go in from the right, and the others are going to parachute in, and then we're going to do X, and then you're going to do Y. Are there any questions?"

> And in the movies, nobody asks a damn question! I'm just flabbergasted! And I'm convinced in real life people tend not to ask questions. They say: "Oh yeah, okay, we'll do that." But me, I would be flooded with questions like "What happens if it goes wrong? or "What if they already know that we're going to be trying to do this?" Or "What's our plan B? What's our plan C? What's our plan D?" I have a whole host of questions that come up to the forefront of my mind automatically, but they didn't always come to the forefront in my mind. I have to practice getting familiar with these kinds of questions.[3]

_____

3. Dr. Gerald Nosich, "How to Improve Your Critical Thinking Skills," interview by Michael Frank, *Life Lessons*, https://lifelessons.co/personal-development/criticalthinking/.

Take Courage

People don't always take kindly to being questioned. Ask too many serious questions of your boss or commanding officer and you may quickly find yourself in some second-rate position. Questioners may be dismissed precisely on account of their questioning, and all the more readily if they are from groups whose questions have traditionally been ignored or dismissed, like children or students or members of marginalized groups or people whose views are out of the mainstream in whatever direction.

Calling out some of the world's naked emperors may even cost you your life. The philosopher Socrates sought answers to questions such as *What is virtue?* and *What is justice?* from the great men of fourth-century BCE Athens—at least those who considered themselves great—but when they could not give adequate answers they ended up so angry that they eventually had Socrates executed for "impiety" and "corrupting the youth."

We are not urging recklessness. Yet sometimes the only thing to do is to muster up our courage and question anyway. A contemporary case in point is soccer star Megan Rapinoe, who has outspokenly questioned sexist and homophobic discrimination in professional soccer, as well as social inequality in the United States, and visibly declined to participate in team celebrations of the national anthem. Predictably, she has been roundly criticized and attacked for this as well, both by people whose politics it offends and by people who think that politics has no place in sports. Yet for Rapinoe the politics is inevitable. *Not* to challenge or question, she says, especially when you are such a visible role model, is also a political act.

Again, there can be consequences. Rapinoe has said that she began protesting during the national anthem in solidarity with NFL quarterback Colin Kaepernick, who had earlier begun kneeling to protest racial oppression in the United States. But while the best athlete on one of the most successful teams in the world (Rapinoe) can speak out without being kicked off the team for her questioning, a good athlete on a good but not great team (Kaepernick) suffered when he did the same thing. Agree or not, we should at least give both of them credit for using the power they have to try to lift up others less powerful. Kaepernick has stated that he felt taking his stand was the right thing to do despite the consequences.

"And What Color Is God, Mrs. Johnson?"

Author and organizer Juanita Brown describes an early experience in questioning—and a moving example of good parenting.

> I am seven years old, in the second grade at Orchard Villa Elementary School in Miami, Florida. Mrs. Johnson is my teacher. She is very religious, in the Southern tradition. I am a small child for my age—skinny, lively, inquisitive. I want to know everything about everything.
>
> Mrs. Johnson holds prayers in the classroom each morning. One day, while everyone is praying to God, I start to wonder what God actually looks like. As soon as the class prayers are over I raise my hand and pipe up in my squeaky little voice, "What color is God, Mrs. Johnson?" Mrs. Johnson turns beet red. She is extremely upset. I don't understand why she's so angry. She grabs my arm and hisses, "Young lady, you are going right to the principal's office and we're calling your mother." She marches me to the principal's office, and they call my mother. I sit in there, terrified, until my mother arrives.
>
> There we are—the principal shuffling her papers, Mrs. Johnson, still looking outraged, and me, getting smaller and more petrified by the minute. My mother comes into the room and sits down quietly next to me while Mrs. Johnson recounts the sin I have committed in asking the obviously impudent question, "What color is God?" during school prayers. My mother listens in silence. She looks at the principal behind her big wooden desk, then moves her gaze to Mrs. Johnson, sitting primly next to the principal. Then she looks down at me, cowering in my seat. She puts her arm around me warmly, smiles, looks up at my teacher again and asks, "And what color *is* God, Mrs. Johnson?"[4]

---

4. Juanita Brown, *The World Café* (Fielding Institute, 2001), 134–35.

"Shall Not the Judge of All the Earth Do Right?"

Speaking of God, some of the all-time riskiest questioning is related—believe it or not—in the Bible. When God proposed to destroy the city of Sodom, the patriarch Abraham could not see the justice of it. Genesis reports that Abraham "went before the Lord" and, well, asked some pointed and surely impertinent questions. He questioned God!

> Abraham drew near and said: "Wilt thou indeed destroy the righteous with the wicked? Suppose there are fifty righteous within the city; wilt thou then destroy the place and not spare it for the fifty righteous who are in it? Far be it from thee to do such a thing, to slay the righteous with the wicked, so that the righteous fare as the wicked! Far be that from thee! Shall not the Judge of all the Earth do right?" (Gen. 18:23–33)

Shall not the Judge of all the Earth do right? Abraham demands. "Behold," he acknowledges, "I have taken upon myself to speak to the Lord, I who am but dust and ashes." Yet he goes right on to repeat this line of questioning, and not just once, but five more times. In his view, justice asked no less. Moreover, God actually granted Abraham's point, and the Bible later says that God "was mindful of Abraham" as events unfolded. Abraham's questions even called God to account.

FOR PRACTICE

2A

Consider the following questions from the standpoint of this chapter. What first steps do you think would be best? Why?

SAMPLE

Question: When will the world end?

Sample strong answer:
I'd start by trying to figure out who is asking. If the questioner is a fundamentalist of a certain sort, the question probably refers to a vigorous debate about the timetable for the "End Times" according to the book of Revelation. Basically it means "When

will Jesus return?" to the participants. Another context might be climate-change predictions, where it means something like "When will current climate conditions shift enough that we can no longer live like we do now?" Both versions of the question assume very specific and very different contexts, and some people might not accept either one. Both debates are also surprisingly nasty.

Comment:
This answer nicely picks out two different meanings of the question and rephrases it in more specific terms. Yet another likely context might be astronomy, where the question probably refers to the eventual explosion of the Sun, consuming all the planets. The question would be asking when this is predicted to happen (not to worry: not for a few billion years).

"The end of the world" is a fraught topic in general. ("Apocalypse" is another term for it—you get the idea.) It seems that people can be captivated, one way or another, by the question of how it all might come to an end—and argue endlessly and angrily with each other too. This is probably what the last two sentences of the sample answer are pointing toward, but the thought could be better worked out. Given how different these worldviews are, is it actually surprising that there is such acrimony? Would we be able to think more clearly if we noted and then avoided trigger words or phrases like "the end of the world" in the first place?

1. Who's winning?

2. What would Jesus drive?

3. What is the most important thing to learn while in college?

4. What would you do with a million dollars?

5. Why do we dream?

6. Isn't evolution just a theory?

7. If Corporations Are People, Why Hasn't Texas Executed One? (bumper sticker)

8.   Why do they hate us?

9.   Is this a great country or what?

10. You talking to me?

11. Are you now or have you ever been a member of the Communist Party?

12. Who cares?

2B

Here are some questions that meant something quite specific in their original contexts—many of them interesting, unexpected, and varied. If you don't recognize them right away, start by finding their original context (this may take a little research). Be sure to consider what the same question could mean in quite different contexts.

SAMPLE

Question: Where's the beef?

Sample answer:

I learned from Ralph Keyes' book I Love It When You Talk Retro (Macmillan, 2009) that this question was first popularized by a 1984 Wendy's advertisement suggesting that Wendy's hamburgers had lots more beef than their competitors'. Whether this was true or not I don't know. Anyway, the ad showed a patron trying to find the actual hamburger inside an oversized bun from a (fictional) competitor. The ad caught on and even inspired a Nashville hit by Coyote McCloud called "Where's the Beef?", also recorded for Wendy's. The question was then seized on in the same year by Walter Mondale's presidential primary campaign to challenge the substance of his competitor Gary Hart's touted "new ideas." Mondale eventually won the nomination, and the phrase went on to become an American watchword, meaning something like "Where is the substance here?"

A strong answer, backed by research, that considers how the original question was used in a quite different context.

1.   Ain't I a woman?

2.   Et tu, Brute?

3.   Who is John Galt?

4.   How many piano tuners are there in Chicago?

5.   Is there balm in Gilead?

6.   Why is this night different from all other nights?

7.   What is the air speed velocity of an unladen swallow?

8.   When there is something strange, and it don't look good, who you gonna call?

9.   If not me, who? If not now, when?

10. Hey Dad. You wanna have a catch?

11. I do not mean to pry, but you don't by any chance happen to have six fingers on your right hand, do you?

12. How shall we sing the Lord's song in a strange land?

2C

How might the following questions need clarifying and/or unpacking? (You don't need to actually answer them to do this exercise.)

SAMPLE

Question: Can you tell if the cats still look hungry?

Sample answer:

My aunt asks me questions like this, and they drive me crazy! Probably she just wants to know if the cats are hungry. Now, I mean. But the way she asks it tangles it up with so many more questions! "Do the cats look hungry?" does not literally ask if they are hungry, but instead asks how they <u>look</u>. Don't cats always look hungry? More, to ask "Do the cats <u>still</u> look hungry?" implies that they (also?) used to look (and be?) hungry. But what if they did not look hungry before, even if they look hungry now? Technically, in that case, the answer to "Do the cats still look hungry?" is NO (right?), because they don't <u>still</u> look hungry, they just look hungry now. And on top of all of this she asks if I can <u>tell</u> if they still look hungry. So technically it isn't even a question about the cats anymore, but about what I can tell about the cats. By then I'm completely stuck trying to figure out what the question even means!!

Comment:

This answer is amusing but also, alas, right on. When you literally unpack the original question, there are tangled layers of questions within it. Which may not really be intended, but literally there they are.

Of course, that may also be a reason not to take the question literally. You could just check the last time the cats were fed and feed them on a schedule. When you answer, just specify the question you are actually answering. "Yes, it is time for them to eat." Or "The cats don't look hungry now." Or "Yeow, Fluffy—that's my finger!!"

1. Why do you look so sad today?

2. Can moons have moons?

3. Is it okay to lie if the lie doesn't hurt anyone?

4. What kind of person would wear *that* tie with *that* shirt?

5.   Is a fish aware of water?

6.   Is it politically correct for a marriage ceremony to say "man and wife"?

7.   How come bikers act like they are exempt from the rules of the road?

8.   Should there be reparations for slavery?

9.   Where is God right now?

10. What is the biggest thing that your religion gets wrong?[5]

11. Should you believe everything you think?

12. Does life have any meaning?

2D

This chapter celebrates the biblical Abraham as a kind of Question Hero because he was willing to question even God when he thought that God was not living up to moral standards. However, tradition also offers another and more challenging story about Abraham. Not so much later, God sends an angel to command Abraham to bind and sacrifice his son Isaac on the altar on Mount Moriah (Gen. 22). This time Abraham unquestioningly prepares to obey, and the sacrifice is only called off at the last moment, when Abraham has already raised the knife. God specifically rewards this obedience too—no qualms.

This story has troubled religious commentators ever since (Jewish, Muslim, and Christian: remember, Abraham is forefather to all three modern Western religions). It seems to be the very opposite of Question Heroism. Check out some of the many commentaries. What do you think is the best way to make sense of the two stories together?

---

5. This question is specifically proposed by Yuval Noah Harari in his book *21 Lessons for the 21st Century* (New York: Spiegel and Grau, 2018), 218.

3

Key Critical Questions

Critical questioning is often labeled *skepticism*—especially when it is not so welcome. It's understandable that people don't always take kindly to having their cherished beliefs questioned. Besides, critical questioning is not always undertaken with much sensitivity to how unsettling it might be. Sometimes it may seem—and sometimes it may *be*—cynical or unduly argumentative. So "skepticism" does not necessarily have a good name.

We suggest thinking of skepticism more positively. At its best, skepticism is simply the recognition that knowledge is not easy to come by. As Chapter 1 pointed out, many things are not what they seem. We need to act accordingly. Look for reliable evidence, check sources, put factual claims to the test, think carefully and persistently. These are basic things—and necessary.

Besides, it turns out that approaching difficult and important matters with a degree of skepticism is not only a good idea, and generally a valuable contribution, but also can be a lot of fun. Some other synonyms for "skeptical" might be *free-thinking, quizzical, curious, inquiring, perceptive, sharp-eyed*. Sound better?

The point is not to mistrust everything, any more than it is to have strong beliefs about everything. In many cases—maybe even most cases—we have no choice but to act one way or another even when we don't have all of the information we would like. Still, let's say you try for maybe *three* good critical questions about the really important things, before leaping—but questions that are sharp, on-point, calm, and persistent when necessary. Let us see what some of those good questions might be.

Questioning Sources

Most of what we believe about the world comes to us from other people: supposed authorities, reference materials, internet news sources, friends, parents, online product reviews, car ads . . . Here are some key questions to ask about them.

Is the Source Knowledgeable?

The most basic requirement is that sources know what they are talking about. You need an art expert to detect a forgery. For the best way to make an angel food cake, ask a chef, or maybe Great-Aunt Bea, whose cakes always took first place at the County Fair. And yes, if you want to know whether global climate change is real, ask actual climate scientists.

Expert sources can still be wrong. As we've said, there is always more to know. The more relevant point, though, is that *non*-expert views are *regularly* wrong. Well-informed sources are almost always a better bet, even when we feel very sure ourselves, and especially when we very much want to believe the opposite.

Note that an informed source need not fit our general stereotype of an "authority"—and a person who fits our stereotype of an authority sometimes may not even be an informed source. If you're checking out student life at college, for instance, students are the real authorities, not administrators or recruiters—though they will be the ones you mostly hear from—because it's students who know what student life is really like. Just be sure to get a representative sample (see below).

Is the Source Reliable?

Sources may be knowledgeable but not necessarily trustworthy. That is why we don't just take suspects' word for it when they claim to be innocent of some crime. Presumably they know very well whether they are innocent or not, but if guilty they have too strong a motive to lie. Likewise it is why we rely (or should rely) more on sources like *Consumer Reports*—an independent organization with a reputation that depends on impartiality and that derives its data from consumer feedback and repair records—than on manufacturers' claims about their own products. The manufacturers don't necessarily have an interest in full or critical disclosure, while *Consumer Reports* does.

Beware of compromised sources masquerading as independent. Industries, political candidates, movements, and the like may set up organizations to front for their agendas—to make them appear authoritative and neutral. "Experts" may even be cited with impressive-sounding credentials, but if you look more carefully they often turn out to be in the employ, one way or another, of the interested parties.

Again: for better or worse, things are not always what they seem. All that glitters is not gold.

Citing Sources

To establish both a source's knowledgeability and reliability, it is usually necessary to cite the source. In this way you guarantee for yourself and for others that there *is* an actual source, for one thing, and everyone can get some sense of how well-vetted the claim is. Peer-reviewed scientific publications, for instance, are not going to publish claims that are merely hearsay or unchecked fantasy. Are you relying on them—or just echoing some random internet blogger?

Citation styles vary—consult a style handbook to find the appropriate format for your purposes, and note that many word processors, including Word, have automated citation generators that allow you to change the citations based on the style needed. All include the same basic information: enough so that others can easily find the source on their own.

Do Reliable Sources Agree?

Cross-check a variety of sources to see if other, equally good authorities agree. Are the experts sharply divided or in agreement? If they're pretty much in agreement, theirs is the safe view to take—and the opposite view is, at the very least, unwise. If one expert is ranged against many, don't bet on a one-off—trust the many.

And if the experts themselves disagree on some subject, reserve judgment yourself. Don't jump in with two feet where truly informed people tread with care. Again, they *could* still be wrong—but what's most likely? And seriously—how would *we* know?

Still, not all disagreement is the same. On any significant topic you can probably find *some* disagreement if you look hard enough, particularly about those things that make a real difference to wealth or power. Worse, on some topics the appearance of controversy may be deliberately created even when there is little or no disagreement among qualified authorities. If you read much of the US popular media, for example, you'd think that climate change is still controversial among climate scientists. But it's not.

Online Sources

To say "I read it on the internet" is only a joke, not a reason. The internet is not really a source at all. It merely transmits other sources. Savvy users know how to evaluate online sources just like any others—with a good many critical questions.

With many websites it may be difficult to tell who or what *is* the source—a red flag already. If you can find the actual sources, are they knowledgeable? Trustworthy? Or are the sites pushing an agenda—trying to sell you something, manipulate your view on some issues by, say, using misleading or highly emotional and manipulative language, poor (or no) data, one-off or phony "experts"? At minimum, cross-check using other, independent websites or question other authorities (e.g., if you are a student, ask your professors) on the same issue.

Remember that even the most deceptive or hateful opinion website can dress itself up to look plausible and even professional. In fact, such sites are deliberately designed to fool us—to make us trust them. Academic book publishers and even most public libraries have at least some checks on the reliability and tone of the books and other materials they collect, but on the internet, it's still the Wild West. You've got to ask and follow up your own questions.

Savvy users may also—cautiously—consult Wikipedia. You can't simply cite Wikipedia, of course, to back up a claim. Wikipedia's intention is to organize and summarize knowledge published in other reliable sources on a subject, and then to point readers to those sources, which articles are required to explicitly cite. Savvy users must also remain watchful—as in any source—for hints (obvious or subtle) of loaded language, dismissive accounts of disfavored views, and the like.

It's certainly true that "anyone can edit Wikipedia," as is often objected. False and defamatory information can sometimes be posted. Subtle biases surely persist as well, and some pages in particular may be prone to tampering and are definitely not reliable. Still, precisely because nearly every Wikipedia article can be edited by anyone, they are also subject to constant scrutiny and correction. Wikipedia's editors sometimes intervene if there is too much contention, and some hot-topic articles are not open to just anyone's editing, but the end result is that Wikipedia's overall error rate actually compares favorably even to the *Encyclopedia Britannica*'s[1]—which (should this be a surprise?) also definitely has an error rate.

Meanwhile, every change is tracked and explained (every page has a complete "View History" tab) and sometimes widely debated as well (check out the "Talk" tabs). What other reference source is so transparent, wide-open but self-correcting? *Really* savvy users might join the work of making Wikipedia still better.

---

1. See Jim Giles, "Internet Encyclopaedias Go Head to Head," *Nature* 438 (December 2005): 900–901. March 2006's *Nature* includes a response from *Encyclopedia Britannica* and a rejoinder from *Nature*.

"Fake News"

"Fake news" is a popular meme today—that is, stories that are circulated with the deliberate intention of misleading or confusing people. It's nothing new, actually. Deliberately false rumors, doctored or made-up reports of great threats or great military victories, and the like have been used to major effect for a long time.[2] Now there is even *fake* fake news: websites that promote such absurd stories that, supposedly, no one could believe them . . . except that people do. (And this is what? A satire of "real" fake news . . . whatever that would be . . .)

Yet a good critical questioner should not often be misled. You know what to do: look to the sources. First of all, what *is* the source? Oftentimes, there is no citable source at all, just rumors or random claims from people who, in fact, probably know no more than we do.

---

2. See David Uberti, "Fake News and Partisan Blowhards Were Invented in the 1800s," *Splinter*, October 6, 2017, https://splinternews.com/fake-news-and-partisan -blowhards-were-invented-in-the-1-1819219085, accessed July 4, 2019; and Keegan Goudis, "Did Fake News Kill Alexander Hamilton?," *Salon*, January 1, 2017, https://www .salon.com/2017/01/01/did-fake-news-kill-alexander-hamilton-false-information -is-nothing-new-but-we-need-new-standards-of-transparency/, accessed July 4, 2019.

Sometimes you might treat the more extreme opinions as entertainment (what if Donald Trump really *were* a puppet of space aliens?) but there is no basis for actually believing them.

When there actually is a source, pose the three questions in this section to it.

Is the source actually knowledgeable? A lot of the fake-est fake news comes from loud, self-certain, and opinionated commentators whose very tone ought to make us distrust them. It sure seems like opinion is all they've got. If your doctors were so full of bluster and self-assertion, would you trust them with your life? Seek out better sources in general. When some source keeps passing on baseless stories, it's time to change channels—literally.

Again: *Is the source reliable?*

And: *What do cross-checked sources and experts say?*

Questioning Generalizations

Does money make you happy? Are computers taking over? Is a vegetarian diet healthier than eating meat? We might want to know. Yet our experience typically gives us just a few examples: two or three super-happy or super-unhappy rich people; a computer that beats you at chess; maybe a vegan octogenarian who swears by tofu. Generalizations in general (!) are ways of trying to move beyond those limits. Sometimes, at least, even from a few examples, we want or need to draw much wider conclusions. But of course—no surprise—critical questions are necessary here too.

Are the Examples Specific and Clear?

Nothing can be generalized from vagueness. A vegetarian friend who sometimes seems a little lethargic is no real evidence in the health department—it's just an occasional impression. A seventy-five-year-old lifelong vegetarian who runs marathons, on the other hand, would be a respectable example—though just one. Likewise, if you are trying to decide whether horoscopes are trustworthy, you need examples of specific horoscopes that actually came true. A vague prediction—"Somebody will be nice to you today"—is not even a start.

Just because a computer can beat me at chess may not prove anything about its real capacities. How good am I? Beating the World Champion, by contrast—though this took massive computing power—was darn persuasive . . . at least about chess abilities.

Are There Enough Examples?

Even when the examples are crystal clear, *many* examples are usually needed to make an adequate generalization. One or a few prove very little. Just because my sister had an awesome experience at Sarah's Spectacular Superstore, it does not follow that you should shop there. Jim Fixx, who was a major advocate of running for exercise and who "wrote the book" on running and ran marathons himself, died at fifty-two—of a heart attack during a run. It's ironic, but it does not follow that he was wrong. Likewise, that a computer could beat the World Chess Champion is a specific and clear example of a computer besting a human, but by itself it does not show that "computers are taking over." That takes many other equally specific and clear examples. (And what do you think: Will computers ever be good at *questions?*)

Does money make you happier? (Than what?) For sure, there are striking examples of spectacularly rich people who have been spectacularly *un*happy. Shall we therefore conclude that money makes you miserable? People do:

> The oil billionaire J. Paul Getty was notoriously unhappy and lonely for much of his life. Entrepreneur and socialite Howard Hughes became reclusive and paranoid, while multi-millionaire pop star George Michael revealed in a recent documentary how his wealth and fame had never made him happy . . . The tales of many lottery winners are replete with envy, spite, and family break-up . . . The misery of the rich is legendary.[3]

Bearing in mind our first question, you'll note that these examples are sketchy and anecdotal, basically one-liners, not specific and clear. More detail and support are needed, starting with citations (How do we find out whether the claims about these billionaires are true?), biographies, careful surveys of lottery winners, both before and after they won the lottery, and so on.

Beyond this, though, an equally serious problem is that this argument only offers a few examples: three super-rich people and a few

---

3. Dayana Yochim, "Money = Happiness," *The Motley Fool*, https://www.fool.com /news/commentary/2004/commentary040120dy.htm, accessed July 12, 2019.

lottery winners. You can probably find three examples of almost anything if you look hard enough—say, very rich people who are spectacularly *happy*. Such a broad claim may be true, but we need a much wider sweep of examples to even begin to tell.

Are the Examples Representative?

Why can't you make a major national product decision based on a survey outside a Best Buy in suburban Tucson? You know: because Tucsonans, or Best Buy shoppers, or Southwestern suburbanites, are only one very small slice of the market. What about rural Idahoans who shop at local hardware stores? Seventy-somethings in St. Louis? Teens in Tallahassee? Your examples must be *representative* of the population you are generalizing about. Market research firms know how to do this—that's why a marketer needs them.

Likewise, you can't generalize about students at your school, say, by just taking your friends or classmates as examples, even if you have a lot of them. Maybe you tend to like outgoing, studious, Ultimate Frisbee players . . . so what about introverts, people who are less studious, football fans, part-timers, or people who can't stand sports? You may have some very large classes—perhaps enough examples purely by the numbers—but they too are unlikely to be representative of your whole school. Maybe they are art history, or microeconomics classes—but what about chemistry or music theater students? Students who mainly take small classes, or who only take classes online? To truly generalize about all students at your school you'd need either a way to ask everyone, or a method for random and representative selection, ranging over all students, ages, class sizes, majors, and so on.

Watch the Rates

Some specific horoscopes actually do prove true. In a class of thirty students or so, for instance, you can usually find someone whose daily horoscope is reasonably accurate. Just as her horoscope said, she won a prize that day, or his girlfriend fought with him. That very day!

Looked at by itself this seems impressive. So maybe there's something to horoscopes after all? But think again. What about the other twenty-nine horoscopes that were completely off, or so vague as to be useless? Even though there occasionally may be strikingly accurate horoscopes, then, the accuracy *rate* of horoscopes is abysmal. Even completely random predictions will be right a few times—one in thirty might be about the likely rate, in fact.

Furthermore, we have a bias for things that are unusual. If you try remembering what you ate last Thursday—assuming last Thursday was a typical day for you—it may well be hard. But if you think about what you had for your last birthday, or in an unusual setting, you are much more likely to remember. And likewise, we are likely to remember the weird events: like when a horoscope seems right on, rather than all of the times it isn't. Or that dream about your mother . . .

We also need to look at what is *not* predicted but should have been. Consider the "prediction-worthy" events of the day, so to speak—Did you win a prize? Did you get food poisoning from dinner?—and ask how many of these, if any, our horoscopes predict. What might *that* rate be? Like, zero?

These points have practical applications. Today many people live in fear of crime or constantly worry over stories of shark attacks or terrorism. Such things do occur, of course, and often are featured on nightly news programs. Without doubt they are awful when they occur. But the probability of any of them actually happening to any given individual—say, the shark attack *rate*—is vanishingly low. No doubt we are preoccupied with the exceptions because they are much more exciting and more memorable than other, far more common ways to die that we really *should* worry about, such as diabetes-related illnesses and heart attacks. The amount of news coverage they get does not have any relation to their actual likelihood.

What if you saw the headline "Woman in Elon, NC suffers from diabetes-related illness"? That's more like *The Onion* than *Buzzfeed*, but it's also far more representative "news."

Are There Counterexamples?

Finally, ask of any generalization if there are counterexamples. A *counter*example, literally, is an example that is the *opposite* of the conclusion: happy rich people, say, or failed horoscopes, or stereotypically human tasks that computers can't even begin to do.

Sometimes a single reliable counterexample completely upends a generalization. European ornithologists thought it was obvious that all swans are white—until black swans turned up in Australia. That was that.

Other times, counterexamples can be a generalizer's best friends, if you ask after them early and use them to sharpen your generalizations and to probe more deeply. The generalization that fast foods tend to be unhealthy is certainly true of many, like french fries and milkshakes and cheap burgers. But *all?* What about some sandwich franchises, which are "fast food" too, but offer fresh vegetables as primary ingredients, meats and cheeses as add-ons, and nothing is deep-fried? (And, of course, as usual, we need to ask: healthy or unhealthy compared to what?) So it seems that the health issue is not with fast food per se, but with certain ingredients and ways of preparing it. What would be a more accurate generalization about this issue, then?

Questioning Explanations

Constantly we are trying to make the best sense we can of experiences or information like these—things that need *explanation*, and often can be explained in more than one way.

"Explaining" in this sense is not like telling someone the rules of badminton or making an excuse for missing a date—that is also a kind of "explaining," but not the kind we have in mind. Rather, it is to infer an underlying cause or motive to some event or behavior. What *explains* your friend's nervousness or why your car won't start, or some crime? We don't see causes directly in such cases. We only see aftermaths: someone's agitation, crop circles the next morning, Mr. Boddy crumpled on the floor of the library. The explanation is our supposition about what went on or is going on behind the scenes: what produced these effects.

Does the Proposed Explanation Fit All the Facts?

Any explanation should account for all the known facts—the sorts of things your mechanic would ask right away if your car won't start. It's no good supposing that the cause is a dead battery if the lights and radio still work. It's no good blaming Colonel Mustard if you know for sure that he was in Kalamazoo on the day of poor Mr. Boddy's murder.

Other things being equal, ask what is the *simplest* explanation that explains all the facts. Start by looking to see if there is a single underlying cause. If you are driving along and all of a sudden half of your warning lights come on (this recently happened to Weston), it is remotely possible that each of them came on for a separate failure that just happened to exactly coincide—but it is *way* more likely that *one* failure caused all of these effects. Noticing which warning lights came on should be a good diagnostic of what that failure might be—or, to look at it the other way around, the fact that certain of your warning lights *didn't* come on is also highly relevant and useful. Already you can narrow down the wide range of likely causes.

Likewise, it's remotely *possible* that, say, the Moon landings were a hoax—something that a surprising number of people apparently believe. Actually, though, the hoax theory explains nothing. (The flag apparently flying in the airless Moon? There's a wire in it, for heaven's sake, as is obvious in the photos and as the TV commentators endlessly explained "way back when.") Even more importantly, the hoax theory can't explain basic facts about the Moon project, like the fact that hundreds of thousands of people over an entire decade would have had to have been involved in such a massive plot, yet not a single one has given it away in the entire half century since—and how likely is that? (Note again that what *didn't* happen is a highly relevant fact.) Plus the Moon rocks the astronauts brought back . . . and the detailed photos from space of tracks and descent stages at the landing sites . . . and on and on and on.

What Causes What?

A correlation occurs when two (or more) things often accompany each other, such as watching more TV and having a lower life expectancy (a true correlation),[4] or sitting near the front of classrooms and higher grades (ditto). When there is one condition or event, the other one(s) are likely to appear too.

You've heard the saying "Correlation is not causality." This is a complex topic, but here we can say that correlation isn't a bad *clue* to

---

4. Steven Reinberg, "Too Much TV May Take Years Off Your Life," *HealthDay*, August 15, 2011, https://consumer.healthday.com/senior-citizen-information-31/misc-death -and-dying-news-172/too-much-tv-may-take-years-off-your-life-655869.html, accessed September 1, 2019.

causality, yet, like other clues, it takes critical questioning. Correlations can be explained in more than one way. Maybe sitting near the front of the room really does improve your grades because you listen better and/or the teacher gives you more credit for being engaged. But it may also be the other way around: students who get better grades tend to move forward.

Or, possibly more likely still, better students—those more interested, engaged, and able—choose to sit near the front to start with. In that case your grades and where you sit are not directly causally related: they are both related to something else instead.

Or all of these factors may be operating at once, and reinforce each other. Maybe good students tend to sit near the front because they know they are more likely to engage there and thus learn more; and teachers, knowing (at least subconsciously) that good students tend to sit near the front, have higher expectations for those students and encourage further engagement from them, leading to better learning and thereby to better grades. It can work both (all) ways at once.

Does the Proposed Explanation Stand Up to Testing?

Test the proposed explanation—and the likeliest alternatives. If you have good reason to suspect that your car won't start because the battery has died, then jump it or replace the battery and see what happens. If you think your friend is nervous because of a test on Tuesday, see how she is on Wednesday. And go ahead—move right up to the front of the classroom and see what changes.

Even more basically, be sure that the proposed explanation *can* be tested. This is another subtle and sometimes difficult point. Beware of the kind of "explanation" that is so vague or slippery that it can be used to account for anything whatsoever. Maybe your car won't start because it has a gremlin—a mischievous small creature who gets inside machines and causes problems? You can test or replace the battery—it's easy to show that the cause is or *isn't* a dead battery. But how can you test for gremlins? (That is, is there any way to show that the cause *isn't* a gremlin?) "Well, it just went and hid again—gremlins are tricky, you know." A testable explanation is one that can be proved or disproved. Only that way, if it survives the test, do you really know you are onto something.

FOR PRACTICE

3A

How might the following claims need critical questioning?

SAMPLE

Claim: Oysters are an effective aphrodisiac.

Sample weaker answer:
I don't eat oysters, they're gross. I have plenty of sex drive, though, so I don't think there is much connection. I do wonder if oysters would help those who don't have as much of a sex drive. I find that hard to believe, because I don't need it.

Sample stronger answer:
I wondered why would anyone think this in the first place? It turns out to stem from a single 2005 study that found that eating shellfish—not specifically oysters—increased levels of one amino acid related to sexual desire—in lab rats (Alicia Ault, "Are Oysters an Aphrodisiac?," *Smithsonian*, https://www.smithsonianmag.com/smithsonian-institution/are-oysters-aphrodisiac-180962148/). However, whether anything can be inferred from this about humans, or oysters either for that matter, isn't clear. Multiple studies, of oysters and with humans, would be necessary to establish a reliable connection.

Comments:
The weaker answer actually misreads the question. The suggestion is not that oysters are the only possible aphrodisiac, or that aphrodisiacs are the only way one can have a sex drive. So the existence of a non-oyster-eating person with a strong sex drive doesn't address the issue at hand. Besides, the example of one person doesn't show much, especially when it's the author reporting on their own sex drive. There's hardly a topic where self-report is less reliable.

    The stronger answer directly addresses the question, gives plausible reasons for skepticism, and draws on research (again, hurrah!) to show that the buzz about oysters is, alas, a bit overexcited. (Sorry about that.)

1.   King Arthur really existed.

2.   This marriage is truly a match made in heaven.

3.   The Bermuda Triangle is haunted.

4.   Vitamins are good for you.

5.   Christmas was originally a pagan holiday.

6.   Natural gas fracking does not cause earthquakes.

7.   Marriage in the Bible is between one man and one woman.

8.   Life on Earth began 3.5 billion years ago.

9.   Beyoncé is a vegan.

10. Oil and auto companies conspired in the 1920s and 1930s to take over and destroy the streetcar industry in American cities.

11. Vaccines do not cause autism.

12. I love you.

3B

What would be the best sources to support or refute each of the following claims? Explain your choices. Remember that some of these claims may need clarifying first.

SAMPLE

Claim: There is life on Mars.

Sample answer:
Planetary scientists, basing their conclusions on data from Mars landers and orbiters. The data would need to be accessible to all and

---

the conclusions presented in peer-reviewed science journals and widely accepted by other well-informed astrobiologists.

Comment:
Sensational claims are constantly made about alien life (probably second only to sex). Some people scour the tens of thousands of photos of Mars now available, and parade anything that looks even slightly odd as evidence of Martians. And of course certain kinds of artifacts on Mars, clearly indicated in multiple photos and otherwise unexplainable, *would* be evidence of Martian life. But some puzzling shadows or unusual shapes are not such evidence. It seems that the signs are likely to be subtle, bacteriological or chemical for instance, requiring scientific judgment and argument. (And there are a few hints, but nothing decisive as of this writing.) How exactly we determine what is "life" would also be a useful question. Lifeforms (and non-lifeforms) elsewhere might be quite different than life on Earth.

1. You are a genius.

2. I am a genius.

3. Your university is the best university in the United States.

4. The paleo diet is better than vegetarianism.

5. Volvos are exceptionally safe cars.

6. Electric vehicles cost two-thirds less to drive.

7. Marijuana is harmful to the brain.

8. The pyramids could not have been built by ancient peoples without the help of extraterrestrials.

9. It's obvious that other animals feel joy and pain just as you and I do.

10. It makes sense to play the lottery.

11.   There are safe ways to store nuclear waste until it is no longer dangerous.

12.   Freud was right.

3C

What examples might be offered for or against the following generalizations? How plausible do you think each is, in the end? Why?

SAMPLE

Generalization: The best things in life are free.

Sample answer:
I think most people would probably agree that "the best things in life" include things like love, friends, health, good work, and happiness. If "free" means "not something we have to buy," then it seems safe to say that most of these are at least partly "free." All of them take effort, and none are guaranteed, but they are not primarily things we buy. We have to achieve and sustain them in other ways.

Comment:
This answer is careful to be clear about the meanings of key terms. It offers likely supporting examples and proposes a reasonable evaluation of them. It might also consider possible weaknesses in the generalization. For example, maintaining or restoring health certainly can cost money for medicine or physical therapy or healthy foods. And some people's happiness does depend significantly on being able to buy certain kinds of things. Cross-cultural data on happiness suggest there is a link, up to a certain income, between money and happiness. Certainly a homeless person would, quite typically, be happier in a house or apartment they could afford. It's complicated!

1.   Most traffic accidents are caused by people in too much of a hurry.

2.   The only certainties in life are death and taxes.

3.   "A stitch in time saves nine." (Or is it "If it's not broken, don't fix it"?)

4.   Cat lovers are totally different types of people than dog lovers.

5.   "Power corrupts, and absolute power corrupts absolutely." (Lord Acton)

6.   Most religious biologists believe in evolution.

7.   Red cars get pulled over more often for speeding.

8.   Members of Congress are always resigning or being forced out for sexual misbehavior or influence peddling. But what do you expect, they're politicians!

9.   Dental X-rays today are totally safe. Your exposure is no more than you get flying across the country.

10. "The arc of the moral universe is long, but it bends toward justice." (Martin Luther King, adapted from Theodore Parker)

11. A North Carolina woman recently bought a lottery ticket just to prove to her husband that buying lottery tickets is a waste of money. Instead, she won a million dollars![5] This joke's on the lottery skeptics, isn't it?

12. All generalizations have exceptions. (Does this one?)

---

5. Mary Beth Quirk, "Woman Buys Lottery Ticket to Prove It's a Waste of Money, Wins $1M," Consumerist, updated October 31, 2016, https://consumerist .com/2016/10/27/woman-buys-lottery-ticket-to-prove-its-a-waste-of-money -wins-1m/, accessed July 13, 2019.

3D

Question the following proposed explanations. If you think there is a better alternative explanation, state what it is—and explain what makes it a better explanation.

SAMPLE

Argument: Vegetarian children tend to have higher IQs. This proves that smart people give up meat.

Sample strong answer:
Apparently children's vegetarianism and above-normal IQ are somewhat correlated, but the underlying story is not clear. Maybe IQ affects diet, but it also might be the other way around: maybe diet affects IQ (meat makes you dumb?). Actually, it seems to me most likely that another factor affects both: social class. Vegetarianism is more common in middle- and upper-class families, whose children are also likely to have educational advantages so that they do somewhat better than average on IQ tests (which are still likely class-biased).

Comments:
In short, maybe diet doesn't affect IQ *or* vice versa, but social class influences both. This kind of indirect causality is sometimes called "Common Cause." An interesting suggestion.

In this and many such arguments, it is also a very good idea to check out the alleged correlation itself. It's confidently stated here, but how well and widely established actually is it? One British study from the 1970s shows a whopping 10-point difference in childhood IQ between adult vegetarians and non-vegetarians.[6] Among other things, this would tend to show that intelligence influences diet rather than the other way around (because the IQ difference was measured in childhood but the vegetarianism is in adults). More recent data from the United States, on the other hand, show quite a small correlation, and only for women. In this case, there is probably not enough data to be very confident about the claimed correlation.

---

6. Catharine R. Gale, Ian J. Deary, Ingrid Schoon, and G. David Batty, "IQ in Childhood and Vegetarianism in Adulthood: 1970 British Cohort Study," *British Medical Journal* 334 (2007), 245.

1.   Since so many people have pets, we must have a deep need for animal companionship.

2.   On average, people who go to college make more money than those who don't. Going to college raises your income.

3.   If the Bermuda Triangle isn't haunted, how do you explain the strange disappearances of so many ships and planes in the area?

3.   Hitler and Stalin were prominent atheists—and look at the immense suffering they caused. The implications are obvious.

4.   If aliens aren't real, why are there such widespread reports of UFOs and alien kidnappings?

5.   Keeping a gun actually makes you less safe. Data clearly show that houses with guns are more likely to have gun-related deaths.

6.   Pot rots your brain—just look at the stereotypical pot-head.

7.   The oil companies are sitting on special secret patents that could drastically reduce or eliminate the need for oil and gas to run cars. Otherwise, why don't we have them already?

8.   OK, Creationists, explain all those fossils!

9.   Among many other reasons we know that the Moon landings were no hoax is that the film technology required to fake astronauts in Moon-gravity motion did not exist in 1969. Rocket technology had been rapidly developing for decades for military purposes, but film had none of today's computer-based capacity to create special effects. Ironically, at the time it was actually easier to send people to the Moon than to create a film faking it.[7]

---

7. For development of this argument, see https://earthsky.org/space/video-moon-hoax-not?utm_source=EarthSky+News45d79-1c55c7f3cd-393761977, accessed July 13, 2019.

10. People who watch Fox News are mostly conservatives. People who read *Slate* tend to be liberal. Therefore, politically biased media shape their users' political views.

11. Economic downturns tend to cause increased anti-immigrant sentiment. Just look at the United States and Europe today.

12. Orbiting observatories have detected a star whose brightness varies in irregular ways that suggest some kind of interference from complex shapes in between. One intriguing explanation is a so-called alien megastructure, a massive artificial construction in space partially enclosing the star.[8]

---

8. Check out Tabetha Boyajian's TED talk "The Most Mysterious Star in the Universe," at https://www.youtube.com/watch?v=gypAjPp6eps.

Key Expansive Questions

We come next to questions that enable us to think more creatively. Sometimes they even have to nudge or even sharply elbow us a bit. They often sparkle and delight as well. These kinds of questions open up unexpected new opportunities and possibilities—that is why we call them "expansive"—and represent a very different but equally vital way of thinking through questions.

Exploratory Questioning

Imagine a group or team in which the first reaction to any new idea is "It will never work." It's a declaration, a pronouncement—no expansiveness there. Besides, people say, the boss won't like it. And if it's really such a great idea, why hasn't someone thought of it already?

The first step to a more creative or expansive way of thinking is to replace this kind of negativity and closure with openness and curiosity. Instead of asserting that it could never work, try approaching the very same topic with a question. Just for a moment, at least, consider other possibilities. _Could it work? How could it work? If it were possible, how could we do it?_

You may still be skeptical. But skepticism is not what is needed in this case, at least not right out of the gate. Try for a more welcoming, open-ended, exploratory attitude. How would you really know if there are any possibilities until you have (seriously) looked for them?

Try out a question like _In what ways . . . ?_ That is, instead of "X isn't possible!," you could ask _In what ways might X be possible?_[1] Verbally it may seem a small thing, but conceptually it is a great leap. "X isn't possible!" is a categorical rejection—you aren't going to think another second about it. By contrast, the question _In what ways . . . ?_ reframes it as an opening of possibilities.

---

1. Following problem-solving guru Edward DeBono's suggestion in his book _Serious Creativity_ (New York: HarperCollins, 1992) and elsewhere.

"People would never do this!" Really? *In what ways might people start to do this?*

"I couldn't possibly sleep overnight in a tent!" Really? *In what ways might you be able to sleep overnight in a tent?*

"Modern societies need strong national governments." Really? *In what ways might modern societies not need strong national governments?*

Cat or Dog—or . . . ?

A key guideline for *brainstorming* is to welcome all new ideas without immediately focusing on the likely difficulties and problems. Another key maxim is to seek out a wide range of potential sources of ideas, and then actively free-associate from there. Even crude and obviously unrealistic ideas, passed around the room, may evolve into something much more focused, and meanwhile they may spark new ideas and even better questions.

If you are thinking of getting a pet, it might seem natural to assume this means a cat or a dog. But suppose you brainstorm other options. How far could you go if you actually set your mind to opening the largest number of possibilities?

Haul yourself off to a pet store, maybe. Besides cats and dogs, usually there are some other pet options too: fish, rabbits, lizards, gerbils, snakes. How about checking out a zoo or aquarium too? Lions, tigers, bears? (We don't recommend this.) How about an octopus? A ferret?

You might do something similar without leaving home. Review some different parts of the world and think of the animals associated with them. Australia—kangaroo? Costa Rica—sloth?

Another fun prompt would be to try a children's bestiary book, one often exotic animal per letter. Anole, Ferret, Quokka, Yak, Zebra? Or you could sign up with animal fostering services and just see what you end up with. Yet again, "digital pets" are all the rage in certain demographics.[2] Could they be for you?

---

2. We don't necessarily recommend these either, but it certainly has been enlightening to follow up this lead—which more or less makes our point. Check out https://www.quora.com/Why-do-people-adopt-virtual-pets and http://www.lostgarden.com/2005/06/nintendogs-case-of-non-game-that.html.

You may still end up with a cat or dog. Then again, maybe you won't. Either way, do you notice how wide (and delightful) a sense of possibility immediately opens up once you begin to pursue it methodically? There's the power of exploratory questioning.

Generative Questioning

In general, expansive questioning calls for playfulness, curiosity, associative thinking, even a little forcibly twisting and recombining ideas. It asks us to watch everywhere for hints and suggestions—for anything we encounter that can stimulate new thinking.

Asking Around

Your problem or issue is probably not unique. Other people have also tried to make better marriages or invent a better mousetrap or solve the Fermi Paradox. So a first and basic move when looking for unexpected alternatives and new directions therefore is simply to *ask around*: that is, to pose the issue or problem as a question to other people, both next to us and far away. *How has the issue or problem been dealt with elsewhere and else-when?*

Ask friends and strangers alike, people very different from you as well as old acquaintances. Read strange books. Look around online. Again, the point is not to instantly produce workable solutions. The point *is* to free up your thinking, to brainstorm from any number of unexpected and perhaps, at first, seemingly unpromising starting points—perhaps even to find some possible allies and collaborators in the process.

American voter turnout is nearly the worst among world democracies. How do other countries do better? Well, it turns out that many have elections on Sundays, or make election days national holidays, so that voters are likely to be off from work, whereas the United States holds elections on Tuesdays, in the middle of the workweek. Come to think of it, it *does* seem more logical to have elections when people are most able to vote, right? Some other democracies also have laws that *require* voting—interesting, but what about more positive incentives?

Asking around, you may also discover alternative voting practices right here at home. Local decision making often requires attendance at meetings where issues are openly discussed—which is quite different than being bombarded by misleading political advertisements and then voting in private, possibly never talking over the issues with anyone at all. Some decisions, like the Iowa caucuses that are so important in presidential primaries, require people to actively dialogue with others with different views. Think of that! Any wider possibilities in it, you think?

Reversals and Opposites

Thinking "in the box" has a usual or preferred or expected direction and pre-organized elements. For creative provocation, you can methodically reverse all of these. Loosen things up, flip the expected directions, think opposites, transpose the constituent ideas.

For example, an expected way to improve things is by speeding them up. This is what much technology tries to do. A *reversal* would be to think about how to usefully slow things down. Eating, say. A Slow Food movement already claims 80,000 members in one hundred countries, devoted to biodiversity issues, new types of food growing, and reclaiming the sheer pleasures of eating. Now how about, maybe, slow travel? There are surely some fine business opportunities here too. There are slow movies as well, like a surprising viral film of a train trip in Norway in real time: the film is just footage of a train moving through the stunning landscape, in real time, for more than seven hours.[3] And people love it.

Most of the world's peoples learn more than one language, but most Americans know only one. Standard ways of worrying about this issue focus on how we can become more bilingual, which of course is fair enough. But how else might we approach the issue?

Ask some wilder (reversed or opposite) questions. Say, *What if we all became monolingual?* That might suggest a shared single language. This might also remind us of various invented universal languages (though typically intended as easily learned universal *second* languages) like Esperanto, Interlingua, and Ido—today all easily learned online, by the way. Are there possibilities here?

Or again, *What if we didn't speak any language at all?* Once again, be careful not to reject such a question out of hand—just take it as a way to prompt brainstorming. A "language" of symbols and signs, for example, perhaps again a universal complement to our first languages,

---

3. Nathan Hellar, "Slow TV Is Here," *The New Yorker*, September 30, 2014, https://www.newyorker.com/culture/cultural-comment/slow-tv, accessed July 14, 2019.

might be way easier to learn and use. It's already partly real in instructions for product use in multiple countries, for one thing, as well as in sign language and in emojis. How could we go further with this?

Plussing +**+ +**

Periodically we give some of our students the task of rethinking the question of traffic around our small but car-intensive campus. One particularly sensible response is to remake the campus to encourage biking and walking and discourage driving: narrowing the roads in favor of bike paths, putting in sidewalks where presently there are few, maybe banning first- and second-year students from having cars, and so on.

Fine ideas. Yet they have one foot still "in the box," wouldn't you say? They're a little too easy and predictable.

Good, we said, but now *stretch*. Walt Disney famously called this "plussing," meaning to take the idea to the next level, and then the next. Instead of just creating a few more bike paths and slightly narrower roads, *What if we took out the roads entirely?* Turn them into bike paths and walkways. Or again, instead of merely creating some non-car options, let's make them attractive, compelling, as wonderful as possible. Don't just build bike paths, then—put them on skyways, along rushing streams, paint them in neon, light them with sparklers. Invent new kinds of bikes. And let's not just put in sidewalks, but create sidewalk food stalls and walking cafes or dance festivals or, who knows, open-air matchmakers or tutoring services. *Now* we're talking!

Magic Wand Questions

Yet another thoroughly enjoyable and powerful method of creative questioning invites us to make a big leap at the very start. *If you had a magic wand and could solve this problem in any way you wanted, what— specifically—would you do then?* In short: *What would be a perfect solution?*

Once again the point is not to immediately come up with a practical proposal—you won't—but to give yourself a new kind of prompt, a creative stimulus to your thinking. This time, instead of slowly working your way out of the "box" with a series of small next-step questions, you ask after "perfection," pushing yourself *way* out of the box right at the start. *Then* you can figure out how to work back toward realism.

Thinking about what to make for dinner, for example, the question invites us not to simply rummage around in the fridge and settle for some mash-up of leftovers. Instead, get out of the fridge and start with the ideal. *What do I really want for dinner?* Then we can ask how we might at least get something like a "perfect" meal using whatever is available. Or maybe you'll realize that you need to just bag it and go out . . . and why not invite a friend?

What would be a perfect adaptation for coastal cities facing rising seas? Wave a wand over New Orleans, for example, and what might we hope for? Maybe a city that . . . *floats?* No problem with rising waters if the city rises along with them. Already, it turns out, many seaside cities have floating neighborhoods. How could they be expanded into whole cities?

Inviting Novel Associations

Really stuck? Try this: start questioning from a *completely random* prompt. Odd as it may seem, here the randomness is the key. It immediately gives you a novel and unexpected set of associations—easily breaking you out of whatever "box" you may unknowingly be stuck in . . . if you let it.

The prompt itself can come from anywhere: walking down the street, chance words in a conversation, a film, a dictionary, a textbook, a mystery, a dream. There are even online random-word generators for this purpose. Best is a source with a varied and rich vocabulary—a classic novel, maybe—but in a pinch you can even take words from billboards along the freeway, or by turning on talk radio for two seconds, as we sometimes do if we are trying to think expansively about something while we are driving.

The US divorce rate is 40–50 percent for new marriages, surely *way* too high. Recently Weston challenged one of his classes to use the novel-association method to figure out how we can do better. To generate prompts in this case—and to make the point that they can truly come from anywhere—he brought in the current issue of our university's student newspaper. Here is a brief account of what happened then.

From an article about the food service, students first plucked the word *soup*. Hmm, they said, this does not seem promising. But don't prejudge it, Weston urged. Prejudging prompts is a really good way of putting yourself right back in the box you are trying to get out of. Just give it a try.

What does soup make you think of? Soup kitchens, someone answered. But what could soup kitchens have to do with marriage? Well, what *could* it have to do with marriage?

What if we promoted service work as a way of finding good partners? someone finally ventured. Service work, such as helping in soup kitchens, often takes commitment, patience, inventiveness, she said—rather like making a long-term relationship work, building a home, raising kids. Besides, it would be great for the soup kitchens, and it would also mean that people would bond over more important and durable values than dinner or movie dates.

Other students chimed in. What if the couple made a permanent commitment to that particular service work? What if family and friends made wedding gifts to the soup kitchen or shelter? What if the wedding party were a weekend building a Habitat house? Or couples could get involved in wilderness trail maintenance or fostering animals, or take the lead in other challenging community service.

These are all first-rate ideas—and how likely would we have been to have thought of them without the help of *soup*? (Notice also the repeated use of "What if . . . ?" questions.)

Next we randomly found the word *again*. Pretty bland? But *again* suggests repetition, so . . . *What if you could (or even had to) get married again . . . that is, more than once?* Could we imagine something like renewable marriage, then—that is, couples recommitting to each other? Some students noted that recommittal ceremonies already exist. It turns out that such ceremonies have been widespread in Italy for decades, and have been known even in the United States since the 1950s. Who knew? Now, what if we made more of them? Mightn't marriage be more romantic when you get to propose and marry all over *again*? Some couples might not continue: the result would be a kind of no-fault divorce, but a lot less trouble and perhaps pain. Others, surely, would rise to the chance to choose each other all over again. Which could be beautiful indeed.

An even wilder and seemingly less promising random word was *bet*. Hmm ... Could people somehow bet on marriages? What would this look like? Maybe when a couple gets engaged a firm could set up an anonymous betting option on their likelihood of staying together? Sometimes people call off their engagement and then hear from their friends what a bad idea it was in the first place. "Why didn't anyone tell me sooner?" But we know why: they were too love-besotted to listen, and besides it's not polite. Anonymous bets could give a lot more truthful information—the bettor's money is on the line—and early enough to make a difference.

We don't know how realistic this last idea is, but it sure is creative. More to the point, would the class ever have thought of it without *bet* as a random prompt? We bet not ...

Long-Lever Questions

Activist and world traveler Fran Peavey used the term "long-lever question" for even more expansive or transformative questions: questions that invite us to rethink fundamentals.[4] Questions with some serious leverage. Here are three kinds of questions with such long "reaches."

What Are the Underlying Interests?

Officially, say, you want a pet. But this, like any choice, is made for certain reasons, with more basic goals or interests in mind. Pet owners tout emotional benefits such as companionship, attachment, non-judgmental affection, and physical touch. Pets are fun too, and bring some variety to our lives. For some couples they are a way of trying out their suitability as parents. A good friend of ours even got a dog in order to meet women (though he came to love dogs too).

Long-lever questions reach back to these basic goals. They do not stay with our immediate preoccupations with pet options, but invite us to look for *companionship* options, *fun* options, even *meeting-romantic-partner* options—interests that might also be met in different and perhaps even better ways.

---

4. Fran Peavey, *By Life's Grace* (Gabriola Island, BC: New Society Publishers, 1993), esp. 87–93.

If your goal is mainly to have some other-than-human presence in your life, for example, birdfeeders might be another (and much less demanding) way. Or if caring for animals is your prime concern, maybe you could work at an animal shelter, help train guide dogs, or join a fostering program. If some variety in life is your interest, maybe you should try iCat. If necessary, invent it. If attachment, or just plain old fun, are your real interests, maybe making a few new human friends would be a more rewarding path.

You could also ask some direct questions about what you really need or want. *What am I looking for in a pet? What are some of the finest animals that I've known? What made them so special? How could I bring animals like that into my life again?* Questions like these may move us way beyond cats and dogs, again, and maybe even beyond pets.

Long-lever questions also apply to—indeed may be key to resolving—social conflicts. People's official positions on controversial issues like abortion and gun control are often sharply opposed. Consider the underlying *interests* of the different sides, though, and common or compatible goals may well come into view.[5] In the abortion issue, for example, *both* "life" *and* "choice" are prime interests. Almost all of us value both highly. Unfamiliar and even shocking as it may be to point out, this is a fundamental agreement. Where do you think we might go if we took *that* as our starting point?

How Can the Problem Be Headed Off?

Another long-lever question is *How might we keep this problem or issue from coming up in the first place—at least in so difficult a form?*

If you are tempted to eat too much chocolate or play too much online chess, the best strategy may be to remove the temptation. Don't just work on your willpower (though there is nothing wrong with that either)—you can also stop bringing chocolate into the house. Remove the chess sites from your menu bar. You could still get chocolate, or an online chess game, if you really wanted to, but you can certainly make it a little tougher for yourself—and often that is enough.

It seems to be hard to get people to recycle. The usual response is still more recycling programs, sometimes with more penalties for not recycling. A longer-lever questioning would ask about how to reduce

---

5. We adopt the language of "positions" and "interests," as well as the general approach here, from Roger Fisher and William Ury's helpful classic *Getting to Yes* (New York: Penguin, 1991).

the need to recycle in the first place. Suppose we made things that bio-degrade so fast you can just put them in the garden for a few days? Or maybe they have other attractive uses, like building blocks, collectibles, or toys? Maybe even make them *edible*. Instead of the ever-present (and non-biodegradable) Styrofoam, imagine take-home containers that you eat for dessert. Where is the problem of recycling then?

Could the Problem Also Be a Solution?

On the other hand, if (say) you find yourself playing a lot of online chess, you might also consider taking up chess as a serious avocation or even vocation. It's not necessarily a problem at all—maybe it's a *hint*.

In general, we label situations as problems when something comes up that threatens to disrupt or complicate the plans we are following. But the very label of "problem" can be a trap, blinding us to the possibilities in those very situations. This leads to our last long-lever questions: *Are there ways in which the seeming problem might actually be welcomed? Are there opportunities in it? For what?*

Think of any problem as a complex state of affairs that, however undesirable in certain terms, also creates new opportunities. Each new emergent issue or problem highlights resources and opens up possibilities that were not on the board before. For example, power plants produce, among other things, heat. Big plants build huge cooling towers and/or locate where they can discharge large volumes of hot water. The heat, in short, is considered a problem—a waste. But doesn't heat have uses? Why consider it "waste"?

We could instead pipe the hot water or steam into homes for heat. This is already done in Scandinavia, where people speak of "cogeneration." The power plant is actually conceived as a heating plant as well—it's a resource and not a problem at all.

As workplace technologies replace more jobs, don't we have an opportunity to reduce the workweek, rather than cut more jobs while overloading those workers who remain? Or again, as the number of aged people increases, shouldn't we be actively asking what aged people can *do*, rather than what must be done for them? Child care? Staffing museums and libraries? Reimagining the long-term future?[6] What are we waiting for?

---

6. This is an example of "asking around" as well. Look at the roles of the aged among native peoples, for instance, and you may see precisely this: part of their role is to hold the *future*. They're the ones whose perspectives are long enough to do just that.

FOR PRACTICE

4A

Reframe the following questions in more open-ended and expansive ways.

SAMPLE

Question: If you hate your job so much, why don't you just quit?

Sample strong answer:
First I would check to be sure that you really do hate your job, rather than just assuming that you do. Then naturally, if so, I'd ask why and in what ways. Maybe from the answers it would be clear that you really do need to change jobs, or alternatively maybe it would be clear that with one or two adjustments you already have a fine job, so the question is how to make those changes. If the situation really is hopeless, then I'd ask what kind of jobs you would like instead, and how you might be able to find them.

Comments:
As posed, the question sounds belligerent and impatient—and "just quit" is surely not helpful advice by itself. The alternative questions in the sample answer are usefully exploratory. It would also be helpful to ask what you most want in a job (i.e., not yet asking about specific jobs, but in general) before beginning to look at specific job options—or seeking other ways to meet some of the goals of having a job.

---

1. Where are all the good men out there?

2. Isn't everyone just out for themselves?

3. Should we impeach?

4. Who discovered America?

5. How can we even think about spending a hundred billion dollars to go to Mars when there are so many unmet needs right here on Earth?

6. If that's really such a great idea, why hasn't someone thought of it already?

7. Which is worse, failing or never trying?

8. Why can't we cure the common cold?

9. Is cynicism ruining your love life?

10. Why can't anyone in this house ever manage to put things away where they belong?

11. If you don't love your country, why don't you just leave?

12. *What Kind of People Should There Be?* (title of an early book on genetic testing and "neuroethics")

4B

Use expansive questioning to generate new ideas about the issues or problems below. Share your lists. Include a brief note with each new idea explaining how you arrived at it.

SAMPLE

Issue: Boredom

Sample weaker answer:
Obviously we need to find ways to be less bored. The answer is to create some excitement and interest in things. Just sitting around being bored is not getting you anywhere. Maybe you should get up and go for a walk or something. Moving your body might get your thoughts off the boredom. At least it's healthier than just

sitting, and maybe after a while you will find yourself thinking about something else.

Sample stronger answer:
One of my friends never seems to be bored, so I started by asking him. "Do something—anything—with young children," he said. Or with a dog. Following up with "novel association" from there, I thought of washing a dog (oh boy); going for a run or swim (from the idea of running with a dog); making some music (as I let my eyes wander over to my old CD collection); and cleaning the room (ditto: Why do I even have all those old CDs?).

Then I went to the internet for more prompts. My very first hit was an article called "96 Things to Do When You're Bored"—who knew?—including ideas like writing someone special a love letter (this also made me think of writing a card to long-lost relatives, or a letter to the president); cooking something special; going dancing; exploring my neighborhood on Google Earth; memorizing Morse code (or learning Dutch, or the Army alphabet, or . . .) and "updating your gadgets" (or why not just getting rid of most of them?). Not to mention really exotic things like skydiving, or WWOOFing (traveling the world working on organic farms—a real thing). I find that just thinking about such things puts a quick end to boredom.

Comment:
The first answer's one specific suggestion is to go for a walk, which is fine, and for many people really may help. It's a start. Still, so far this answer seems so "off the top of the head" that someone could easily think of it without serious effort or using any of the tools offered in this chapter. Aim to go much further.

The much better second answer suggests not just walking but running, swimming, walking (or washing!) the dog, or Google-mapping the neighborhood . . . concrete and venturesome suggestions, calling on specific creative thinking methods such as asking around and novel association. It also conveys a lovely spirit of expansiveness just in narrating the process. More and more options seem to open up for the author—it's as if once she starts free-associating, she can't stop.

1.   What if time travel were possible?

2.   How can we make school more exciting and interesting for all students—starting with your own class and classroom, right now?

3.   Invent three completely new forms of art.

4.   What might be two new practical ways to overcome racial prejudice?

5.   How can we improve our system of government?

6.   What can be done to help overloaded young parents?

7.   What can be done about homelessness?

8.   Invent a completely new game or sport.

9.   Invent a completely new business.

10. What are three creative answers to the vulnerability of coastal construction (houses, roads, power lines) to hurricane damage (winds, washouts, storm surges)?

11. What would it take to completely end littering?

12. An old song goes: "Ain't gonna study war no more." OK, so what then?

4C

Done with 4B? Are you sure?

Good—now go back and do it again. Use all of the kinds of questioning strategies in this chapter to generate *even more* new ideas about these problems . . . and let us just say: you absolutely *can* do it. Again include a brief note with each new idea explaining how you arrived at it and which strategies you used.

SAMPLE

Issue (once again): Boredom

Sample strong answer:

Well, this was interesting. I started by trying to "plus" some of my answers from 4B. The idea of writing a card to long-lost relatives made me think of other unusual kinds of writing. How about finding foreign pen pals? (There are websites that will set you up.) Or trying my hand at poetry? (I see that our local weekly has a poetry contest . . . why not?) The idea of long-lost relatives prompted me to think also of getting genetic testing to find out who they might be. Today many of my friends are discovering all sorts of unsuspected ancestors and relatives—definitely not boring either.

A long-lever question would be <u>How can boredom be headed off in the first place?</u> If you are bored in your college classes, maybe you have the wrong major. Or shouldn't be in college right now in the first place. (Travel! Work!) Then again, could boredom sometimes be a good thing? How about . . . a business opportunity? Maybe if I got really good at getting "un-bored," I could go into business as a boredom coach. Or start a pay-per-call boredom hotline (you'd call up and hear wild jokes, creative suggestions, etc.). Actually, this would be quite possible . . . and not at all boring work, either.

Comment:

Many more ideas were possible after all, eh? This answer gets quite inventive and even fun by the end.

By the way, some research suggests that bored people are actually more creative.[7] The "wandering mind" of the bored person naturally free-associates, the authors suggest, leading to the kinds of creativity we have been practicing. Budding boredom coaches should be sure to remember this too. Boredom isn't always bad even for the bored person!

---

7. Sandi Mann and Rebekah Cadman, "Does Being Bored Make Us More Creative?," *Creativity Research Journal* 26, no. 2 (2014): 165–73.

4D

Develop two long-lever responses to each of the following issues.

SAMPLE

Issue: Off-topic computer use in class

Sample strong answer:

Students get pulled into distractions in class mostly when the class does not hold their full attention. You don't surf the web or text your friends when you are doing something totally engaging. So one long-lever solution to the problem of off-topic computer use in class is to make the classes a lot more engaging. Make them faster-paced, involve students more. From what I hear of my sister's classes in law school, everyone pays constant and close attention all the time, because anyone in the class may be called on at any moment to be cross-examined on the readings or on the discussion to that point. It's pretty tense, but it is also how it is in court—that's the point. You don't want your lawyer doing anything off-topic in court either.

Might there be some opportunity in student computer use in class? Suppose teachers tried to make use of it, rather than suppress it? Some classes might call on students to do on-the-spot research online and report to the class. There are also many web-based exercises and simulations that classes might do together. Class notes, or even discussions running at the same time as the class proceedings, could be compiled in a Google Doc that is displayed on the classroom screens.

Comment:

In-class computer use is typically considered a problem, but framing it as such tends to block us from any other way of viewing it. As the last paragraph of this sample answer suggests, we might at least consider reversing direction entirely and actually build a pedagogy around it, rather than always try to ban or suppress it. Surely the availability of massive amounts of information and other computer-based aids should often be a huge *advantage* in the classroom.

1. The uncertainty of weather reports

2. "Paper or plastic?"

3. Political campaigns with little money

4. The appeal of drugs

5. Vegetarian versus meat diets

6. Driverless cars

7. The decline of basic public civility

8. Traffic jams

9. Fund-raising for public radio and other good causes with "free rider" susceptibility (i.e., once they're out there, people can use them without paying for them)

10. Plastic pollution in the oceans

11. The cost of higher education

12. Terrorism

4E

When Bloch-Schulman taught a draft of this book, students all remembered the plussing strategy, often using plusses in their written work as a mnemonic (a method to remember something). This is not a surprise. Research shows that students learn better by dual coding, that is, moving or translating an idea between different types of expression, for example, by describing a photograph in words or trying to draw an image of a philosophical idea.

With that in mind, we challenge you to work out at least two good, simple images, like the plusses we used above, to "code" the following topics and strategies described in words in this text. Share your images in class with others to see which best capture the idea and which best help everyone remember it.

We have left several pages blank at the end of the book for your doodles. You might start your drawings and visual ideas there as you read or review. In addition, we would be happy to see your drawings and also would like you to be able to share your images with others. Please send your ideas to us through the webform at www .hackettpublishing.com/thinking-through-questions-support. We will select some of our favorite ideas to post on the book's website.

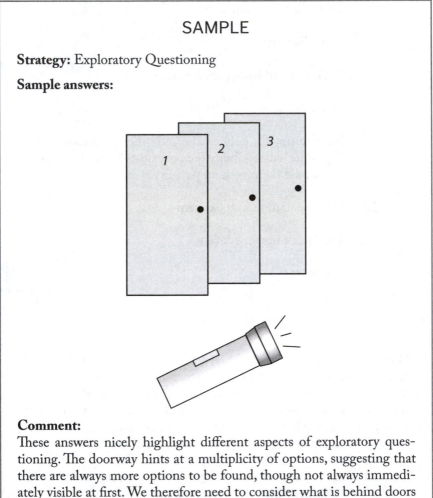

SAMPLE

Strategy: Exploratory Questioning

Sample answers:

Comment:
These answers nicely highlight different aspects of exploratory questioning. The doorway hints at a multiplicity of options, suggesting that there are always more options to be found, though not always immediately visible at first. We therefore need to consider what is behind doors number 2 and number 3! The flashlight icon highlights the activity of searching, of exploring and taking careful notice of what might be easily overlooked or usually left "in the dark."

1.   Our definition of questions

2.   Why study questions?

3.   Clarify intentions

4.   Clarify terms

5.   Take your time

6.   Persist

7.   Take courage

8.   Questioning sources

9.   Questioning generalizations

10. Questioning explanations

11. Generative questioning

12. Long-lever questioning

Key Philosophical Questions

Still other sorts of questioning are among the chief jobs of philosophers. Let's survey a few.

Questioning Assumptions

One key kind of philosophical question has to do with the assumptions behind our ideas or practices. *What do we normally take for granted*, philosophers will ask, *that may need to be thought through, named, and questioned?*

Often you can start a philosophical conversation just by asking thoughtful *What?* or *Why?* questions.

"What is your major?"

"Business."

"What is a business major?"

"A major in business studies the way businesses work and can work effectively, why they succeed and why they fail."

"When does a business succeed?"

"When it makes money for its shareholders."

"Why do we take making money to be the (only?) goal of businesses?"

Here the simple question "What is your major?" opens a series of probing questions about how our society is organized. The repeated question *Why?* is not just for young children.

Basic assumptions are not always easy to notice, which is why philosophical questions can sometimes be surprising or even unsettling. For example, people sometimes say things like "She died too young." Sad as death may be, this way of thinking reflects certain norms and assumptions. One is the idea that we all somehow deserve to live a long time. A philosophical question might be *Do we? Why do we assume that we all somehow deserve to live a long time?*

Put another way: What if we didn't make that assumption? Maybe instead we could think of life as a *gift*, which we are lucky to get to keep at all. In that case we might feel less robbed or heartsick, and maybe more grateful for the time that we, and she, did get. In addition to making death more bearable, this way of thinking might also make life sweeter, don't you think?

From another angle, we might be led to wonder at the disparities in death rates between the genders and between different racial and socioeconomic groups. In this sense you could argue that some of us really do "die too young" after all. What might be done about this?

A Philosophical Recipe

How do you make an apple pie from scratch? Normally this question does not seem hard to answer. Just get some apples, brown sugar, and . . .

But wait, said astronomer Carl Sagan. This question makes a few assumptions that it might be useful to highlight. If we are really making an apple pie from *scratch*—that is, really from *nothing*—don't we first need to make . . . a universe? After all, the apples and the sugar . . . and the farmers and the soils and the water and the sunlight . . . have to come from somewhere too. Don't we have to go all the way back to the beginning?

Didn't think of *that*, did we? Probably we just wanted a recipe. Still, as Sagan reminds us, there are cooks and then there are astronomers. Even seemingly small and entirely practical questions can be surprising and revealing, and provocative too, if we take them without some of the usual assumptions.

Freedom Through Questioning

When we identify underlying assumptions, the point isn't necessarily to replace them immediately. They may be quite reasonable. All the same, questioning them can be very helpful. It makes us realize that our first or automatic or socially expected ways of thinking are not the only ways to think. It may open our minds and remind us of more expansive possibilities.

The child who asked *Why is the emperor wearing no clothes?* calls out the emperor's fakery and the people's hypocrisy. Had there been a philosopher nearby, she might have gone on to ask something a bit more risky: *Why should we have emperors at all?* Maybe it's not just this one emperor who is "naked," but the whole *idea* of rule by emperors in the first place?

Radical, eh? Kings and emperors once claimed to be anointed by God to rule on earth as God is supposed to rule in heaven. It was philosophers of the Enlightenment who led the way in, yes, questioning this supposed "divine right of kings"—helped out, for sure, by the constant misadventures of kings and emperors of the time. *Why have kings at all?* these philosophers started to ask. At first the question was unheard of. Yet the rest, as they say, is history—including the history of the United States of America.

Who Speaks for Earth?

Onondaga Faithkeeper Oren Lyons tells of a dramatic moment when the Iroquois nation took the world stage to question certain basic assumptions of today's political discussion.

> We went to Geneva, the six nations, the great Lakota nation, as representatives of indigenous people of the western hemisphere . . . "There is a hue and cry for human rights," they said, "for all people," and the indigenous people asked, "What of the rights of the natural world? Where is the seat for the Buffalo or the Eagle? . . . Who is speaking for the waters of the Earth? Who is speaking for the trees and the forests? Who is speaking for the Fish, for the Whales, for the Beavers, for our children?"[1]

1. Oren Lyons, "Our Mother Earth," in *I Become Part of It: Sacred Dimensions in Native American Life*, ed. D. M. Dooling and Paul Jordan-Smith (New York: Parabola, 1989), 273.

Questioning Meanings

Other philosophical questions concern the meanings of terms, especially at the points where a great deal depends on certain concepts but ordinary understandings lose their way. Dictionaries by themselves cannot tell us whether unequal access to health care is unjust, for example, or whether atheism is a religion. For that we may need to think through questions like *What is the true meaning of Justice?* or *What is a Religion, anyway?*[2]

Socratic Definitions

One method for seeking out the "true meaning" or "essence" of things in this sense comes from the fourth-century BCE Athenian philosopher Socrates, briefly introduced in Chapter 2.[3] Socratic questioning begins by considering *clear cases* of whatever it is we are trying to define. Working to define "Bird," for example, we might list robins, herons, and hummingbirds. Then we ask, *What is the common feature in these clear cases?*

We might try defining Birds as "flying animals." But are *all* and *only* Birds flying animals? Actually, no. Penguins and ostriches are birds, but they don't fly. Bats and mosquitoes fly, meanwhile, but are not birds. Therefore, some other feature must make the essential difference: something that robins, herons, and hummingbirds have in common with penguins and ostriches but not with bats or mosquitoes.

Ultimately, it turns out, having feathers is what distinguishes Birds from non-birds. Birds are *feathered* animals. This definition gives us a way to draw a clear line between Birds and non-birds, so that the unclear cases can be cleanly and plausibly sorted out. (Were pterodactyls birds? On this definition it turns out to depend on whether or not they had feathers—and they did. So: yes.[4])

What Is Democracy?

Suppose you are wondering whether having elections is enough to make a system Democratic. Let us try using Socratic questioning to help decide.

Again we'd begin by noting clear cases. In Periclean Athens, an assembly of all citizens, even five or six thousand of them, directly

---

2. When we focus on a concept such as *justice* or *religion* in order to investigate its true meaning or essence, we will capitalize the word: Justice, Religion, etc.

3. Worth noting: the Socratic method is a lot more than simply asking questions—though obviously we are not against that either.

4. For more detailed information, check out https://www.livescience.com/24071-pterodactyl-pteranodon-flying-dinosaurs.html.

decided matters of importance to the city by majority vote. New England town meetings end with votes. Modern representative democracies—countries like Great Britain, Japan, India, Israel, and Costa Rica as well as the United States—elect members of Parliament or Congress by voting, and those bodies in turn typically make their decisions the same way.

Still, just as flying might not be *sufficient* to make something a Bird, voting alone is arguably not sufficient, by itself, to make a decision procedure or system Democratic. One reason is that not everyone may have a vote. Athens, for example, limited citizenship to free males. Modern democracies, by contrast, are founded on the idea that everyone affected by a decision ought to have a voice in it— though it is an ideal still to be fully realized. So if voting is essential to a Democracy, we at least need to add that everyone (at least every adult?) must have a vote.

Another problem is many dictatorships and authoritarian countries also have elections. Many even claim to be Democracies for this reason. Typically, though, they have only one option, with a yes vote very strongly expected. Or candidates need to be preapproved by the rulers in power. Or there are choices, but they are limited to trivial differences. Once again, we would not call these countries truly Democratic, even though they have much better voting turnout than we do.

Democracy, then, seems to require truly competitive elections between candidates with significantly different positions. And there is still more to the story. In a truly competitive system, people need to be genuinely free to disagree, even fundamentally, while all enjoy well-established political and civil liberties, a rule of law that applies fairly equally to everyone, with government powers checked by other actors such as a free press and non-governmental organizations. There is much more to say about all this, of course—there are whole books on the subject—but we can at least conclude that true Democracy requires a lot more than voting.

Questioning Socratic Definitions

On the other hand, this kind of questioning does not always produce a clear definition. Sometimes, unclarity or disagreement may go too deep. Exactly *what* more than voting does Democracy require, for example? Or the things in question may only partially fit the definitions. Most democracies are imperfect . . . but they are still Democracies, right?

Change is part of the story as well. Socrates never imagined evolution, for example. Part of our uncertainty about birds may be that it really does seem that flight is part of the essence of a Bird . . . even though some birds don't fly. Still, they evolved from birds that *did* fly (even penguins!). That's probably why feathers themselves evolved.

Likewise, democracies have developed beyond the original conceptions. Today there are new challenges like the outsized influence of money and of new internet vulnerabilities on elections, and it's not clear that older definitions of Democracy give us a clear direction for answering them. It is partly up to us what direction our democracy will go in the future.

Still, Socrates' method for thinking through questions remains vital. Working from clear cases, trying to draw fairly sharp, useful, and non-arbitrary lines between what counts as an X and what doesn't— these tools help make our thinking rigorous and sharp in turn. Even imperfect tools can be kept sharp, and do real work.[5]

Big-Picture Questioning

The aim of much philosophical questioning is to relate our beliefs to each other: to make them more consistent, more mutually supportive, better and more clearly organized, and ideally better founded as well. The aim, we could say, is a fuller and more consistent "big picture."

You are a teacher, say. You have your favored and familiar ways to teach. But these in turn involve many assumptions and commitments: about what is most important to pass on to students, about what it is to learn and know things, and about how young minds develop. And what about joy in learning?

A philosophical approach, as we have been saying, would draw out and probe those assumptions. You'll want to ask how well-founded they are, for one thing. But there is also more. You'll also want to aim for a thoughtful consistency between your ideas, and between your ideas and your methods. If joy in learning is your main aim, for example, then to the extent you are able, you surely want to de-emphasize rote learning of information. Or again, if you are a strict disciplinarian,

---

5. Some philosophers even argue that philosophical questions are what they call "essentially contested"—meaning that there is no non-controversial answer to the question of the true nature of ideal things like Democracy or Love or even Philosophy itself. Still, they favor asking the questions. Keeping them alive as well as open is, in their view, the task of Philosophy.

is it because you believe that children are essentially wild spirits that need to be tamed in order to become (as the phrase goes) productive members of society? If that doesn't sound quite right, on the other hand, what *do* you think about human nature? And mightn't your answer in turn suggest alternative ways of keeping students on track?

Who *are* you, finally, as a teacher? A purveyor of information? A "guide on the side" as students find their own ways? Or something else? These are not questions you might have been encouraged to consider in depth in education school—or if you did, the course was probably called "Philosophy of Education." Certainly they are the big questions!

Moral Consistency

The famous Golden Rule requires us to make the same moral judgment about a situation regardless of what is our role in it. For example, if you think it is alright for you to tell white lies to smooth social interactions, then you should not get incensed when other people tell you white lies. *What would you think if someone did exactly the same to you?* is one form of this kind of question.

Generally, though, mere consistency by itself is not enough. Philosophers look for our beliefs to *cohere* in a deeper way: to fit with and support each other. Again: the Big Picture must make sense as a whole. This is what we mean when we speak of having a "philosophy of life," so to say: basic beliefs and commitments that *hang together*.

Take for example the question of our relation to other animals. There is some uncertainty about the degree to which other animals suffer, but generally we recognize their capacity to feel pain and fear, as well as affection. One troubling aspect is that this goes both for animals to which many of us open their hearts, such as cats and dogs, and others that we confine and kill for food or entertainment usually without a second thought, such as cows and pigs.

The pointed question is *If we would never kill and eat our cats, say* (though there are places in the world where people do), *how is it that we do so with cows and pigs, or confine monkeys or bears or dolphins in zoos or use apes for medical experiments?* More generally, then, how *should* we relate to these other creatures? Might things have to change quite dramatically if we think this question through all the way? If so, we'd better get on it, right?

Many philosophers would say that working out such a consistent ethic is a lifelong project—never entirely done, because of course new situations are always arising. Or to put it the other way around: to be a philosopher is always to be working on it.

Thinking Through Hypothetical Questions

Philosophers also have certain distinctive and inventive ways of thinking about such Big Picture questions. One of these is through *hypothetical* questions.

Case in point: we could, hypothetically, put ourselves in other animals' places and see how things seem to us then. Would our treatment of them still seem just to us if we were in *their* shoes (paws, claws . . .)? One way to do so is to suppose that aliens have taken over the Earth. Maybe they're fairly nice folks too—just like we think we are—except they have the habit of raising and killing humans for food, on a massive scale, as well as using us for medical experiments, drug tests, entertainments such as zoos and circuses, and the like. A few "human liberationists" among the aliens campaign against these practices, but for most, they are just natural and familiar—the aliens have always eaten and otherwise exploited "lower beings" and most of them have trouble even imagining that there could be any problem with it. (Sound familiar?)

No one is saying that such aliens are actually likely to show up. Let's hope not! For purposes of thinking through questions, though, it doesn't matter. The point of the hypothetical scenario—also often called a *thought experiment*—is to focus questions of consistency and coherence. Really the question is *Is our present treatment of so-called lower animals actually justified? Could we consistently object to the aliens' treatment of us while continuing to exploit other animals as we do?*

In the hypothetical case there might be good answers. The humans might be able to argue that we have more in common with the aliens than with other Earthly animals, and therefore should be treated as fellow moral beings rather than food. Then again, maybe not. Or maybe we have some commonalities but not others . . . so, which count? (And what relevant commonalities do other animals have with us?) The point is that figuring out consistent answers will take some hard and careful thinking—and maybe in the end require changes in our own actions toward other animals, perhaps from a new perspective of sympathy as well.

Extreme Questioning

An even more radical kind of philosophical questioning thinks through the ultimate bases of our beliefs and values. *How do we know—anything? Is there anything that we can really be sure of?*[6]

The seventeenth-century French philosopher René Descartes began by trying to discredit absolutely everything he thought he knew, in order to see if anything at all could survive the most radical rational skeptical onslaught he could mount. In the end he discovered that only one thing—his knowledge of his own existence as a thinking thing—could survive even the most persistent and powerful deceiver (note that this is also another kind of hypothetical questioning). From that seemingly bare starting point, though, he thought he could prove the existence of a (non-deceptive) God, who in turn endowed us with senses that give us true knowledge of the world, as long as they are used properly.

Descartes' argument was tricky to pull off, to say the least, especially since God could not be made responsible for all the ways in which our experience falls far short of delivering reliable knowledge. Other philosophers wanted to base certainty on Reason. All too often, though, the deliverances of a philosopher's Reason turned out to be local prejudices or overgeneralizations from limited experience. Later philosophers, taking this limit to heart, argued for a more moderate and practical skepticism, or what the eighteenth-century British philosopher David Hume called "modesty and caution" in our beliefs.

The eighteenth-century Prussian philosopher Immanuel Kant took the opposite tack. We can be sure of how things must appear to us, Kant held, but not because we can really grasp the world "out there." Instead, we carry certain pre-existing, internal "categories," such as the ideas of Time and Cause, into the way we experience the world in the first place—a little like the way water takes the shape of whatever container it is poured into. Which means that the *real* world is in some sense utterly inaccessible, but nonetheless we can be sure that what we experience will take certain shapes.

Except . . . not necessarily. Even the categories that Kant thought were fixed and universal features of the mind turn out not to hold in

---

6. The next paragraphs briefly mention some central figures in what philosophers call "modern" (by which we mean from about 1640–1800) "epistemology" (the theory of knowledge). There is an immense philosophical literature on these questions. For fairly accessible overviews, you might start with the Wikipedia articles on "Empiricism" and "Rationalism."

all human experience. Meantime, though, Kant's idea that the mind plays an active role in the construction of experience has endured, shaping much of the philosophy that followed right up to the present.

Questioning Extreme Questioning

All of this is an exciting story (for philosophers at least). If you want more of it, though, you'll have to study philosophy in some detail. Please do! Here, though, in the spirit of questioning, we close with a few philosophical questions about these kinds of questions themselves.

The twentieth-century American philosopher John Dewey challenged what he called the "quest for certainty," like Descartes', in favor of a more open-ended and experimental approach. Let us prioritize *inquiry*, Dewey urged—an open-ended and evolving process—over *knowledge*, which suggests something more fixed and settled. Scientific theories can be our model here: extremely powerful and sweeping generalizations about the world that at the same time are understood to be tentative and quite possibly incomplete in major but as yet unimagined ways.

In short, maybe we just do not have to *know*. The world might not actually allow the sort of nailed-down, final answers that the Extreme Questioner demands. Dewey's experimental attitude might even be extended to ethics—to ideas of right and wrong. Maybe we can only continuously learn better what best serves the good—even as our conceptions of the good are themselves in flux and open to learning and change.

Many varieties of contemporary philosophy also insist on the necessity of choice and action to create and re-create meaning. Existentialists adopt it as a test of authenticity: can we embrace the necessity of making our own meanings? Critical theorists today look at *who* makes the meanings: what meanings are enforced upon others, usually to their detriments, and how meaning-making can be wrested away from the powers that be.

Here we can only repeat that the very asking of these questions, even when "extreme" and even when no answers are forthcoming, is itself a valuable thing. Philosophical questioning can get us past habitual assumptions, everyday and probably fairly local beliefs supposed to be true of the whole world for all time, as well as beyond various kinds of fatalism, as in "there is nothing to be done." In their place: liberating doubt, the challenge to remake the world, a sense of possibility, and even (dare we say) wonder.

FOR PRACTICE

5A

What are some likely assumptions in the following practices or statements? What kinds of philosophical questions might come up when you think more about them?

SAMPLE

Practice: Buying health insurance

Sample answer #1:

Buying health insurance assumes that at some point in the future you are going to need it. In other words, the assumption is that you can't count on health. This seems to be true even though we often live as though we <u>can</u> count on it (for example, by doing unhealthy things, or not exercising enough, etc.) . . . until it's too late. Maybe if we did not have insurance we'd take more care not to get injured or sick or run-down in the first place.

Sample answer #2:

Literally, the term "health insurance" suggests that health itself is something we can buy. Whereas really what we are trying to cover the costs of is medical care . . . which might or might not restore health. Nothing against <u>medical</u> insurance, but we might be better off thinking of health itself as a kind of gift, rather than a commodity. Maybe then we'd protect it better too.

Insurance is a kind of gamble, isn't it? We pay a rather large amount of money in order to shield ourselves if really huge medical expenses come along—which they might or might not. Not everyone might make this bet—a point made by critics of the tax mandate in Obamacare, who argue that it's not fair to require everyone to buy it. Anyway, we know that a number of us will have those huge medical expenses, but we don't know who, exactly, so we pool manageable amounts of money for the use of those whom Fate strikes with otherwise unmanageable needs. This is why the names of insurance companies often include the word "Mutual." In a certain way it's actually rather beautiful. (I didn't expect to be saying that.)

Comment:

Answer #1's point about not counting on health is also made in a different way by answer #2. It's on target. However, answer #1's main claim could be more precisely thought through. Not everyone is going to need insurance money (or, more exactly, many of us are not going to get more out of health insurance than we put into it, especially when we count foregone interest). Indeed, if we did, the industry couldn't be profitable—whereas in fact it makes such large profits as to be, well, questionable to some.

Answer #2 is stronger than #1. For one thing, #2 makes a more accurate point about the need for insurance. For another, its suggestion that we might think of health as a gift, rather than a commodity, is a more philosophical way of putting something that #1 still seems to be struggling toward. Answer #2 then goes insightfully into some deep (even "beautiful," believe it or not) assumptions behind insurance as such.

1.   Fast foods

2.   "I don't see race."

3.   "Without music life would be pointless." (Nietzsche)

4.   Sport hunting

5.   "Two wrongs don't make a right."

6.   "No pain, no gain."

7.   Throwing stuff "away"

8.   "May the best team win!"

9.   "It's a dog-eat-dog world."

10.   Speaking of dogs, dogs are a man's best friend, right?

11.   "He got his just reward."

12.   "Why do they hate us?"

13.   What is the right amount of water to drink every day?

14.   "Be All You Can Be!" (US Army slogan)

5B

Can Socratic definitions of the terms in bold help answer the following questions? (Remember that sometimes definitions in the law or in a dictionary may help you, but none can be taken uncritically.)

SAMPLE

Question: What is true **Friendship**?

Sample strong answer:
I would define Friendship as mutual care between yourself and another person, based on personal experience of your and their feelings and thoughts. I distinguish Friendship from mere acquaintance (like so-called "friending" online) because we usually think that a friend is more than just someone we meet or enjoy in passing. We have to know the person fairly well. Mutuality is important too: we wouldn't say that we're friends with people if we care for them but they don't give a hoot for us. It has to go both ways.

Comment:
This answer picks out care as the essential feature, plausibly specifying that Friendship requires mutual care, based on experience. It explains itself by twice pointing to clear cases of what we'd usually consider friendship (or not).

This definition is mostly concerned to distinguish Friendship from mere Acquaintance, which might be the difference between "real" and "not real" friendship. A way to develop it further would be to also distinguish Friendship from Love. (What do you think?)

1. Is coffee a **Drug**?

2. Why aren't GMOs (genetically modified organisms) **Natural**? Or maybe they are?

3. Is decent health care a **Basic Human Right**?

4. When is a **Joke** not a joke?

5. Speaking of joking, when does joking about sex turn into **Sexual Harassment**?

6. What is true **Patriotism**?

7. How about true **Love**?

8. How about true **Peace**?

9. What does **National Security** really require?

10. When are we truly **Free**?

11. Can we usefully define **Happiness**?

12. What is **Terrorism**?

5C

Consider each claim below. If you were to hold or commit to that belief, what other beliefs are you likely to also have to support to have a coherent "philosophy"? That is, think about the Big Picture in each case. What larger and more general philosophical questions might each claim raise?

(Note carefully: the question is not asking if these are true or false beliefs, merely what they probably imply and what kinds of questions they raise in relation to other beliefs.)

SAMPLE

Claim: We should only eat dolphin-safe tuna.

Sample strong answer:
For one thing, to believe this we'd have to believe that "dolphin-safe" really is better for dolphins. Apparently the "safe" tuna nets are built so that dolphins can escape from them. But do tuna fishers conscientiously use them? Is compliance well-monitored? In short, can we trust the label?

We're so concerned about dolphin safety. But obviously dolphin-safe tuna nets are not "safe" for <u>tuna</u>! So a Big-Picture question is <u>Why is it OK to save dolphins but kill tuna, who are aware and intelligent creatures too</u>? Plus, tuna fishing apparently threatens not just dolphins but all sorts of other fish and sea life killed and discarded in the course of tuna fishing. Most industrial-scale fishing methods cause massive ecological damage to the oceans (Jacob Hill, "Environmental Consequences of Fishing Practices," https://www.environmentalscience.org /environmental-consequences-fishing-practices). We seem to be distinguishing a few animals as morally important while treating the rest, not to mention the oceans themselves, as ethically irrelevant. How does this make any sense?

Comments:
This answer raises sharp questions, and there is some research behind it, which we always appreciate. It can go deeper still. As to the first point, for example, a little more research would tell you that there is a fair controversy behind dolphin-safe labeling, which gets into issues of how far we can trust the production and regulatory system in general. From there, one might also ask, Is informed consumerism enough? Do our buying choices make (enough of?) a difference? And if not, what might? Might a concerned person need to do more than change what kind of tuna they buy?

The second point is about moral consistency. It's again a deep and involved issue. What general moral principle might tell us that it is morally required to save dolphins, but not tuna? Or the oceans themselves? There's a lot of room for philosophical questioning here. And what if killing tuna *is* as wrong as killing dolphins?

1. Don't Postpone Joy! (bumper sticker)

2. Computers can't have human rights.

3. Atheists must have some secret pain that causes them to reject God's love.

4. The goal of prisons is to rehabilitate wrongdoers.

5. Assisted suicide is morally wrong.

6. A UFO with aliens aboard crashed in Roswell, New Mexico, in 1947 but the government continues to try to keep it secret.

7. Corporations are not people.

8. Magic is real.

9. Anyone can succeed if they try hard enough.

10. Gender is socially constructed.

11. True forgiveness is impossible.

12. One person can only do so much.

5D

A philosophical bumper sticker:

DON'T BELIEVE EVERYTHING YOU THINK

On the one hand, we have a lot of beliefs, about everything from what will happen tomorrow to the sources of the universe (yes?), the color of the wall in front of you, to the love others may feel for you or the love you feel for them, the motives of the other side's politicians, and the best way to make corn bread. On the other hand, we know on a general level that not all of our beliefs are likely to really be true, even if they all feel true to us at the moment. Not only is there no guarantee that we really know the truth about everything, indeed it is pretty certain that we don't, and usually not for elaborate and imaginative reasons like Descartes' but for the simple and common reasons already outlined in this book: our experience is limited, we tend to be just a bit gullible (just a bit!) and jump to conclusions, indulge wishful thinking, and so on.

So we are challenged to take at least some of our beliefs with some serious grains of salt: to maintain what Hume calls "caution and modesty" in our believing. A useful question therefore would be *What do you think you actually know for sure, in the end? And why?*

There may be decent answers. Even Descartes thought there was one certainty, at least—though some philosophers have questioned even that. The text has also suggested that certainty about anything may not be necessary. We can (and maybe have to) live without it. Still, somewhat defanged, it's a useful question. What does it take to be certain? About what can we be fully certain? Or as close as possible? And which of our beliefs, including possibly some cherished ones, might we have to acknowledge as less than fully certain?

Zen Questions

Here is a well-known question from the medieval Japanese Zen master Hakuin Ekaku: *Two hands clap and there is a sound. What is the sound of one hand?*

Notice that Hakuin's question does not ask for the sound of "one hand clapping," as people tend to say. It simply asks for "the sound of one hand." This is much more mysterious. How to answer? You could try clapping the fingers of one hand, but that's not what the question is asking for: it's wondering about something other than another form of clapping. Or, so to say, *What is the sound of no clap?*

As Chapter 1 mentioned, the Zen tradition features questions like these, called *koans* (pronounced **koe-ahns**). A koan can be a question, like this one, or a story that poses a question or that can itself be posed as a question. (Another koan might be: Don't believe everything you think.) Koans are meant to be paradoxical, unanswerable, jarring, and provocative—and therefore, and for just that reason, liberating. Zen students might meditate on one koan for a year or more, trying out various answers—not necessarily in words—with their teacher, who for a time will probably reject all of them. The teacher is looking for some sign that the question has done some sort of transformational work for the answerer.

The general idea is that in our daily lives we often manage to consume ourselves with worries about the past and the future, preoccupations with ourselves, or just distractions of all sorts. Often we take this way of living for granted, as if it were just the nature of life itself, so that we may also feel utterly trapped by it. Koans, the masters say, are meant to break all of this down.

Zen masters would say that the aim of koans is ultimately to awaken us to the world as it is. Their questions force us out of accustomed modes of thought (and of speech and of response to things). They suggest other possibilities. What may stand out are simple moments or things, like the sun pouring in a window some spring morning, so flashingly, jarringly, overwhelmingly alive.

Australian Zen master John Tarrant tells us that "working in this way loosens the knots in the mind." "Usually people think of a creative leap as something like one, two, three . . . six. With a koan a creative leap is more like one, two, three . . . *rhinoceros.*" Koans encourage radical curiosity, Tarrant says; they undermine the habitual reasons and explanations; they tend toward a comic rather than tragic view of life; and, he concludes, they "uncover a hidden kindness in life."[1]

So what *is* the sound of one hand?

There is not any single "right" answer in the Zen tradition. Acceptable answers depend on a particular teacher and student. The challenge to the students is to manifest their understanding—"loosened knots"—with some gesture, using words or not. There are probably as many ways to do this (and even more ways not to do it) as there are Zen students. But what would *any* kind of real answer look like?

We might make some progress if we imagine going through the world one-handed, or with one hand tied behind our back. When we consciously meet the world with our one hand, what does it "sound" like? What is the "clap" of awakening and alertness—not necessarily literally a sound—in that case?

Suppose it were a handshake? Or suppose it is a high-five . . . someone else's hand meets yours, but then the "clap" may be the sheer astonishing fact of the other person, or whatever it is that you are high-fiving together. Or maybe your one hand is waving. Or beckoning. Or stroking a lover's or a baby's skin. Or a cat. (Could "the sound of one hand" be a purr?)

Zen master Edward Glassman writes that some people answer that the sound of one hand is silence, which he calls "at least a breakthrough in realizing that the answer does not have to be clever." He goes on:

> When I ask children this question they look puzzled. Sometimes they wave one hand through the air listening for the answer. Actually, the waving of one hand is one answer to the question. This is hard for some people to understand . . .

> According to Yoel Hoffman in "The Sound of One Hand: 281 Koans with Answers," [an] acceptable answer is for the novice to face the Zen master, take a correct posture, and silently extend one hand forward. This answer embodies much of Zen philosophy. It is immediate, nonverbal, spontaneous, and intuitive.[2]

---

1. John Tarrant, *Bring Me the Rhinoceros* (Boston: Shambhala, 2008), 2, 3, 7, 69.

2. Edward Glassman, "A Paradigm Shift: The Sound of One Hand Clapping," Creativity Portal, March 26, 2011, http://www.creativity-portal.com/articles /edward-glassman/paradigm-shift-zen-riddle.html, accessed July 15, 2019.

But of course, now that you have read that answer in a book, you cannot simply replicate it for the teacher. That would probably be only an imitation without deep understanding. Once again, the question brings with itself a profound openness—not just a variety of answers, but fundamentally a different way of being in the world. Transformation indeed!

6

Questionable Questions

Right about now you might want to take a deep breath. We've been very positive about questions so far. Questions can be your friends—in fact, much more lively, interesting, and empowering friends than we sometimes think, if we welcome them with skill and gusto. But not always!

Certain kinds of questions and questioning are definitely *not* your friends. Questions may also be manipulative or misleading or distracting or destructive—accidentally or by design—and therefore, at times, must be mistrusted and resisted. These are *problematic* questions! We need to know how to think them through too—to know when, and how, certain questions must themselves be questioned.

Loaded Questions

Loaded questions are not asked in a neutral or open-ended way, but instead work to manipulate or coerce certain answers and try to preclude other answers.

Loaded Language

Should the government stop meddling in the medical system and let individuals make their own choices? The language of this question already practically answers for you. No need to actually think—which is exactly the intention. Who wants a "meddler"? Besides, "let individuals choose" sounds like something no right-thinking person could be against. In this way the very phrasing of the question already inclines us toward a *yes* answer—as it is likely designed to do.

This is the simplest type of loaded question: a question that uses emotionally strong and suggestive *terms* to predispose us in one direction or another in response. No side has a monopoly on such language. The question could also be put this way, for example: *Should the government forfeit all efforts to make health care accessible, and abandon even the most vulnerable to the uncaring market?* This time the answer is just as obviously—and uselessly—*no*. No one wants forfeits or abandonment or uncaring acts.

What to do? The best strategy is to try to work out a relatively neutral way to phrase the underlying (real) question. In this case, we might ask something like *How far should the government be involved with the medical care system?* Notice that this question is both neutrally phrased and also open-ended. It invites careful thinking and not just an automatic or gut-level answer. It's a question we can actually *think* with.

Political arguments are a prime place for loaded questions, like *How do we keep welfare bums from eating up our tax dollars?* But many other questions can be loaded too, like *Couldn't you just cook dinner without all the whining?* "Whining" is obviously loaded, but don't overlook that innocent-sounding but suggestive little word "just" either.

Smuggled-in Assumptions

Do you enjoy flirting to get what you want? If you think that's a tricky kind of question, you're right. It puts you in a position where any answer to the question automatically includes the confession that you do flirt to get what you want. Yes it's fun, or no it's not fun, but either way, to answer at all accepts the suggestion that you do indeed manipulate people by flirting.

This is a classic example of another kind of loaded question, this time "loaded" with unstated assumptions in such a way that to answer the question at all accepts the assumptions. However, we need to note that this is not always problematic. If you have come to a therapist to deal with being a manipulative person, for example, then the question may be fair enough, if a little bald. The therapist needs to know if you find your manipulative behavior enjoyable. What you do about it might be very different depending on the answer. In a few contexts such a question might even be quite helpful in prompting a person to better understand themselves and their actions.

Oh, and *How can we keep predatory timber companies from further devastating America's last great wild forests?* This question is loaded in both senses. "Predatory" and "devastating" are both highly rhetorical terms, and the question also requires us to assume that timber companies in fact have acted and continue to act in this way. Unless this is already established, the question ought not simply assume it.

Again, what to do? The first challenge is to notice when assumptions like these are indeed being smuggled in. Then, when needed, you can refuse the question. Point out the assumptions that are being made. Reframe them as questions: *Do* you use your wealth manipulatively? *Are* the timber companies poor stewards of America's wild forests? You can do this even if you share those assumptions. It's clearer and more honest, even so, if the assumptions are upfront and explicit.

"Who Discovered America?"

All sorts of questionable assumptions can be smuggled into questions, sometimes in subtle ways. For example, consider this familiar question: *Who discovered America?*

It seems to be innocent enough. Everyone knows we are supposed to reply "Christopher Columbus," but maybe to show how especially open-minded we are, we'll want to debate some other possibilities, like, say, Leif Erikson. (And did you know about Bjarni Herjolfsson? How about Zheng He?) It turns out this is a matter of some contention. But there is a deeper problem here.

Arguably, the question itself is loaded. The question assumes that it even makes sense to speak of "discovering" America in the first place—if that means bringing America into human knowledge in historical time. After all, for tens of thousands of years before Europeans arrived, the area now known as America had its own people, who obviously knew perfectly well it was there. The question as usually phrased erases them entirely. Even to debate between European or Chinese "discoverers" at all accepts its premise.

What if native peoples had spoken of "discovering" Europe—let alone claimed to possess Europe "by right of discovery"? Today they are more apt to speak of Columbus, Erikson, et al., as *invaders* than discoverers. Is that a fair term—fairer, anyway, than "discoverer"? If not, is there a term that might be fair to both points of view? If not—and there might not be—what does this tell us about the range of diverse perspectives that exist?

False Dilemmas

A specific kind of implicit assumption in a question can be the assumption that there are only some set number of possibilities in the situation or problem being questioned about, when in fact there are probably many more. *Gay or straight? Republican or Democrat? Poor, middle class, or rich?* These kinds of loaded questions are often called "false dilemmas" because they predefine the possible answers in too narrow a way.

What to do? Again, notice the loading, and refuse the question. Keep other possibilities, other options, in view, at least for yourself if not others. *Democrat or Republican?* Well, there are others too, like Democratic Socialist or Libertarian, and mixtures of various views (e.g., conservative on social policy but liberal economically), not to mention centrists and apolitical folks. *A or B? Really? What about C, D, E, F . . . and Q and Z?*

Complex Questions

A question may be loaded because it wraps several quite different questions into one. Logicians often call these "complex questions." Here's one: *Should we get a smaller, safer car?* Several different questions overlap here: *Should we get a safer car?* and *Should we get a smaller car?* For that matter, *Should we get a car at all?* Another key question is *Are smaller cars actually safer?*

What to do? Carefully unpack the different questions, and, again, make the hidden assumptions explicit. Take this one again: *Should the government stop meddling in the medical system and let individuals make their own choices?* There are at least two separate questions here, and less loaded ways to ask them as well, like *Should the government stop regulating health care?* and *Should individuals be able to choose their own health care options?*

Your answers could be different. For example, someone might think that the (federal) government should not be organizing health care, but that health care should be organized on the community level as cooperatives—so, yes to the first question, no to the second. Someone else might think that if people could only get insurance by buying their own individual policies, then only the richest or healthiest would have wide-ranging choices, and that everyone else would have few options or none that are affordable to them—so, probably no to the first question and yes to the second.

Again, really the only decent answer is "It's more complicated than that!" Once you sort out these options and questions a bit, this could be a very interesting and fruitful topic to pursue.

Power Plays

When a question is loaded, the chief problem lies with the question itself. This is why we can often identify loaded questions without knowing much about their context. Another type of questionable question has everything to do with the setting and style of questioning.

Coercive Questioning

Questioners may sometimes have institutional power over answerers, as in an interrogation or cross-examination. This can be reasonable enough, as in a court proceeding, and the questions themselves can be quite legitimate. Usually you ought to just answer, and truthfully and carefully (but courtroom questions can be loaded too—you definitely have to look out). School questions, for example tests, can be fine too. You took the class, after all, knowing it involved tests.

In general, though, we want to minimize the coercive questioning in our lives. Better to have more control over the questions we *have* to answer. In normal life, luckily, it is not exactly mandatory to answer questions like *What is the difference between meiosis and mitosis?* or *Exactly what were you doing on the night of September 5th?* Certainly we do not appreciate being interrogated . . . and even a good biology class might encourage you to pose your own questions (which can take a great deal of knowledge too) rather than just answer someone else's.

Always remember, anyway, that there are other and very different ways to think through questions, especially the ways emphasized in this book: curious, critical, exploratory, and creative ways. Some people may think that questioning is naturally coercive—and it certainly can be: for example, think of the unappealing overtones of the phrase "brought in for questioning." Still, we have tried to show that questioning can be much more companionable and constructive instead. Try for more of that.

Controlling Questioning

Another kind of power play is *controlling questioning*.

> A: What do you think about UFOs?
>
> B: I suspect they're just natural things, like . . .
>
> A: Oh come on, are you going to tell me that all of the thousands of UFO reports are just some weird cloud or bright star? Let me tell you . . .

Even from this brief exchange you can tell that A is aggressively taking charge: interrupting, putting words into B's mouth (B never gets to even begin to explain "natural things") and using loaded terms and ridicule. Grammatically, A speaks in questions (so far), but you can see from the start that "Let me tell you" is the real agenda.

It is not as though natural explanations of UFOs cannot be questioned—as can any other explanations. The point is that the questioning here is a power play, not a genuine coinvestigation. If B plays the game any further, she will be the one who constantly needs to explain and justify herself, and even so A will barely listen.

What to do? Once again, sometimes it is wisest as well as most socially manageable to simply opt out of this kind of questioning. If you stick with it, take some control yourself. Sometimes you may first have to actually name the power play.

> A: Oh come on, are you going to tell me that all of the thousands of UFO reports are just some weird cloud or bright star? Let me tell you . . .
>
> B: Wait! You started this conversation by asking me a serious question, which I was trying to answer seriously. How about you actually listen to my answer before you tell me all about what *you* think?

Questioning to "Win"

Questions can be used in a variety of ways by people who are mostly interested in debating—not to learn or make progress together, but instead to *win*. Debaters may use loaded questions and false dilemmas to take the offensive and keep their "opponents" (one sign of a power play is that it quickly feels like there *are* "opponents") always back on their heels. Other tactics include misstating views in exaggerated or polarized ways, stereotyping the other side ("You're just a . . ."), and pouncing on any small side issues or missteps, oversimplifying complexities while evading the main point.

"Always be against something rather than for something" could be a debaters' motto too. Debaters are apt to run down any positive suggestions, even if tentative and partial. If there is no perfect solution, apparently for them there is no solution at all. Insisting on perfection can be another way to gain a bit of an edge to try to "win"—to put down the other side—but in situations where there is something real at stake it is likely to just leave people stuck.

What to do? Recognizing questioning-to-win tactics is a start—you are less likely to be misled by them. Naming them explicitly may help too.

> C: I am sure you are trying to be helpful,[1] but it feels to me that this kind of questioning is turning our discussion into a battle with personal stakes. We're not on opposite sides in a lawsuit or debating hall here—we should be the *same* side trying to figure out the best decision.

Insist on the complexities of real issues and questions as well. Look for first steps and partial measures, rather than reject them for that reason. Very few problems can be resolved all at once. Sometimes the best motto can be "Good enough for now and safe enough to try." We have found that when we take an exploratory approach and don't imagine that we are going to settle things once and for all, then, oddly enough, we can actually get much further than debaters for whom the question is only what is the final and absolutely "right" position.

Questioning to Stall Change

Questions may also be used to stall or block movement or change. If someone is so minded, they can raise a thousand questions about almost anything, which can nicely gum up the works and stop things in their tracks. Supreme Court nominees, some proposed law or policy or maybe just long-overdue petition, buying a new bicycle or maybe trying the new Mexican place for dinner: *How can we be sure it will work out? What about this? What about that? Could you*

---

1. Actually, you may not be sure at all that the person is trying to be helpful, but it is polite, and sometimes strategic, to give them credit for trying anyway, even if you think they are not. You might be wrong, after all—or they might come around. It's a way to call on their better selves.

answer these two thousand questions, please . . . which no doubt will lead to more . . . ?

In their ways, at times, (some of?) these can be perfectly fine questions. Once again, the problem is how they are used, how insistently, and to what end. Questioning an idea to death can appeal to those who like things the way they are—it can seem cooperative and engaged, while also ensuring that nothing really changes. But it is unrealistic and unfair to imagine that only the new idea or the proposed change is open to question—as if the status quo is not. Don't let an endless questioner make it feel like the only thing insecure is the new idea or proposal. *Not* changing can be questioned too!

What to do? Sometimes it is necessary to put a stop to endless questioning. Again, at least raise the question (!). More positively, you could ask what you really need to know to move forward. Specify—and agree on—a manageable number of key questions, including key questions about the status quo. Try to answer them as best you can, and then, decide.

Questionable Philosophical Questions?

Certain philosophical questions may also be questionable at times. One familiar example is this one: *Isn't everybody really just selfish?* It looks like an actual question, but in practice, we have found that the questioner is almost always already committed to a yes answer, and moreover defends this answer when pressed by defining "selfish" in so broad a way that any deliberate behavior whatsoever counts. Even parents risking their lives for their children, or an artist's sacrifice of every other pleasure for the sake of some great creation, may be called "selfish" in the sense that at least they were what the person chose to do.

If you define "selfish" in a normal sense, though—let's say, roughly, self-*serving* or self-*centered*—then it should be clear that most people most of the time are not "purely selfish." Indeed, so far from it being hard to find an example of a purely unselfish act, it may actually be harder to find an example of a purely *selfish* act. For instance, think again about a parent doing something for their child. Yes, the parent feels good to have helped the child, and that can be seen, in a way, as selfish. But often a parent defines "good for me" and "good for my child" in the same way, so the reason the parent feels good is precisely because what he or she does is good for the thriving of the child. Sometimes it is really hard to even distinguish between selfish and selfless acts.

Another example of questionable philosophic questions returns to the classical line of philosophical questioning briefly introduced in Chapter 5. René Descartes challenges us with the question *Can we be totally sure of anything?* Normally it seems like there are quite a few things that we know: that an icy treat is fabulous on a hot day; that our Sun is a star; that 1 + 1 = 2. But, Descartes asks, can we be *absolutely certain* that we are not dreaming these things (and everything else)?

Maybe not. Some dreams can be very compelling when we are having them. Moreover, even seeming certainties like 1 + 1 = 2 *might* conceivably only be deceptions produced in our minds by some infinitely tricky God. Can we be *absolutely sure* that there is no such "Omnipotent Trickster"? No? Then, the argument concludes, we really cannot be certain of anything—and if knowledge requires certainty (because it might seem that we can't claim *knowledge* of something and at the same time admit that we could be wrong about it), it seems that we actually don't *know* anything either.

Once again, though, it seems to your authors that certain questionable but unacknowledged assumptions are being made. In a practical sense of the word *know*, we don't somehow have to defeat an Omnipotent Trickster to be confident of anything at all. It's true enough that people tend to be too sure of themselves a lot of the time, but it does not at all follow that nobody can ever have any confidence in anything. It may be that the bar for claiming to know something is typically too low, but that doesn't mean that Descartes' bar isn't much too high. There could be a lot of bars in the middle of the two.

And doesn't the context matter here too? We need less certainty about some things than others. If I don't like the taste of peanuts, I might not be bothered by a restaurant server who says he is "pretty sure" there are no peanuts in the sesame noodles. If I am deathly allergic, I would want more certainty!

You could also look at these kinds of questioning as controlling in a subtle way. They succeed only so long as the questioner claims the sole right to ask and define the questions. The minute you question the questioner's assumptions, it all falls apart. Doesn't doubt need as good a basis as belief? Is there better reason to suppose that the entire world is set up as some kind of massive and absolute deception, rather than that things are pretty much what they seem? And can't we (and don't we) live without unquestionable certainties all the time?

Dealing with Questionable Questions

Facing loaded questions or power plays, you do not have to acquiesce or quit the scene. Instead, as we have already been saying, you can resist and try other strategies. As usual (remember Chapter 5!) there are more options than it may seem at first.

Don't Play the Game

One way or another, from the start, make it clear that you are not simply playing the game on the questioner's terms. For instance, you can and should challenge loaded questions or false dilemmas. Unpack different parts of complex questions. Don't just refuse to "play to win"—refuse explicitly, at least when you are in a position to do so.

This may feel impolite or socially awkward. If it does, just keep in mind that there's nothing polite or socially appropriate about questionable questioning in the first place. *They* started it! Anyway, you can usually be fairly polite about it, if you wish—just pointed.

To loaded language: translate a bit.

C: What could be more stupid than eating an all-carb diet to lose weight?

D: I imagine you mean something like What is the rationale for high-carb diets if you are trying to lose weight? It sounds unlikely, I agree, but apparently there actually is something to be said for them. Why don't we look into this a little, rather than just trash the idea because we don't understand it?

To a false dilemma you might say, "That's an interesting question, but don't you think there could be some other and probably better possibilities?" *Dog or a cat? How about a ferret? A yak? An iCat?*

To someone whose main agenda with questions seems to be to tell you *their* answers, you could adapt B's response to the controlling questioning above:

> B: You started this conversation by asking me a serious question . . . How about you actually listen to my answer before you tell me all about what *you* think?

Again, context matters, and pushing back against questions can be risky for some people and in some circumstances. Few students, for example, are in a position to challenge loaded or coercive questions if they come from their teachers. Even if you cannot explicitly do so, though, recognizing that you are being asked questionable questions is essential for your own clarity, careful response, and sometimes just safety. Step away; find ways to challenge questionable questions indirectly. And resolve to be a fairer questioner yourself.

Answer Rhetorical Questions

Just because a questioner asks a loaded or rhetorical question, not expecting or inviting an answer, does not mean that you cannot answer it anyway. Maybe someone flippantly asks, *Who cares?* If *you* care, say so.

Likewise, in the UFO example, when A says, "Are you going to tell me that all of the thousands of UFO reports are just some weird cloud or bright star?", that is an answerable question, if rather loaded. B's spirited answer could be "Sure—you bet." This should at least stop A briefly in his tracks—that certainly was not the expected answer to his rhetorical question—and B can thereby use the momentary pause to actually begin to explain how she thinks that UFO reports *could* be "natural things."

Seriously answering rhetorical questions can even be a fun little exercise.

> C: What could be dumber than eating an all-carb diet if you are trying to lose weight?

> D: Hmm . . . how about an Airbnb in a grizzly bear den? Or maybe denying climate change when you live in South Florida?

C may laugh—or not—but you can hope that he'll ease up a little on the rhetoric after this.

Reverse the Question

Thirty years or so ago, Weston quit eating meat. He has done quite well since then, thank you. But along the way he discovered that one of the challenges of being a vegetarian is constantly being asked *Why don't you eat meat?*

For the most part it is a welcome enough question, often polite and genuinely curious, though for politeness's sake he usually avoids answering it at meals with non-vegetarians. But there are times when it feels more like a power play, putting his diet on the defensive as if it is the only dietary choice that needs to justify itself. Why shouldn't a meat diet be questioned in just the same way? Eventually he learned to turn the question around. *Why do you eat meat?* is a much less expected question, and often leads to quite a different but just as relevant a discussion—sometimes much more provocative.

Henry David Thoreau was imprisoned in 1846 for one night because he refused to pay taxes as a protest against the Mexican-American War, which he held to be unjust and due to slavery. The famous (though likely apocryphal) story goes that his mentor Ralph Waldo Emerson came to bail him out and asked: "Henry, what are you doing in there?" Thoreau answered, "Waldo, the question is what are you doing *out there?*" Good one, Henry!

Reversal is especially helpful when trying to have a constructive conversation with habitual doubters and reflexive skeptics. Point out that it is harder to prove a point than to show the flaws in someone else's. Don't allow relentless skeptics to set themselves up as the unpersuadable judge of any answers. Natural explanations of UFOs or crop circles don't explain the little oddities that sometimes show up? Well, OK . . . and what about the vastly greater oddities and implausibilities that show up if we suppose that aliens are somehow involved?

Ask a Better Question

Always remember: except sometimes in a court of law or classroom, you are not obliged to answer exactly the question you are asked. Especially if the question being asked, or the way it is being asked, is problematic, *change it.*

R: Don't you think that giving money to people begging in the streets is just prolonging their dependence?

S: It could at least help them through the night. But what do you think we should do instead?

S redirects the question to the possibility of actually doing something helpful, rather than letting R's questions remain only an excuse for not doing anything at all, or joining a polemical argument that will probably quickly devolve into political grandstanding. It also shows some real interest. Some other better questions might be *How can we respond in a human way to people begging for money?* (no room for some expansive thinking there?), and also *What might be done about homelessness and poverty as social issues?* (a good long-lever question).

Is any choice ever totally free? Asked modestly, this could be an interesting question, perhaps reframed as *What are some of the major (or perhaps, unsuspected or unwelcome) influences on our choices?*—since it seems that psychologists are always documenting subtle influences that we might not have guessed at. Sometimes, though, it is concluded that no act is free at all—because true freedom, maybe like true knowledge for Descartes, is supposed to be somehow absolute. A philosopher might challenge this assumption explicitly. ("Totally free or else totally unfree." Really? Or another false dilemma?)

Some potentially better questions on this theme might be *How can we make our choices more free? How can we make the most of the freedom we do have, however limited it might be? Are there any influences that have too much power right now?* Or even a reversal: *Is any choice totally _unfree?_* Again, you can probably get a lot further with these kinds of questions than accepting the original question's assumption that the issue is all-or-nothing.

In Whose Backyard?

One essential conversation in our civic life is about where certain unpleasant and potentially harmful things should be placed: prisons, dumps, waste facilities, manufacturing plants that pollute. *Where should the dump [or . . .] go?* is the usual question, and the answer is all too often "Not in my backyard!" Indeed, this kind of answer is so common that people refer to the claim simply as NIMBY.

Of course, people who answer such questions with NIMBY are doing something totally reasonable. Who would want nuclear waste facilities close to their homes? Or a smelly paper mill? Or a toxic waste dump? Who would want the value of their home to plummet? Perfectly reasonable.

But the problem is that they often (though not always) misunderstand the actual practical question. The real question is not *Should we place the waste dump in your backyard?* The real question is *Where should it go?* And the possible answer "not in my backyard" leaves open the equally valid response: then *in whose backyard?* Or, more pointedly, *Why is their backyard any less important than yours?*

These are not happy questions, but we cannot avoid them. We can dodge them, yes, with the predictable effect that the dumps (etc.) will end up in the backyards of the people least able to resist them. In the meantime, the larger question is *If this dump (say) is so bad that no reasonable and reasonably civic-minded person could find it acceptable in their backyard, then what shall we do?* In the long run, justice may require figuring out how to get along without unrecyclable trash in the first place.

Stand Up for Others

As we have noted several times, questioning can be risky, and it can be more risky for some people than for others. The same goes for questioning questionable questions. A final maxim for dealing with questionable questions, then, is to stand up, when you can, for others who may be subjected to questionable questions that they cannot effectively resist or question themselves. This does not mean speaking on behalf of others without their say-so; but it does mean that we have a responsibility to pay attention when they do speak, and to support their questioning of questionable questions when we can.

For example, most Americans know that a person who is arrested must be "read their rights," including the right to remain silent and to have a lawyer present during questioning. We may not know that these are called "Miranda rights" and derive from a 1966 US Supreme Court case involving an accused felon named Ernesto Miranda. But Miranda did not somehow win these rights himself. Others stood up for him—and, ultimately, for all of us who might be subjected to constitutionally questionable questioning.

Miranda was an uneducated Hispanic man with a criminal record when he was arrested for another set of crimes and immediately confessed under questioning. It was not clear, however, that he actually understood his right to a fair trial or legal representation before he confessed. The Question Heroes in this case were certain lawyers and civil libertarians who took his case for free all the way to the Supreme Court in order, they hoped, "finally to recognize the full meaning of the Sixth Amendment." They were the ones who persuaded the Court to curb the often-coercive style of police questioning at the time, which frequently left the accused in the dark about their rights and about the consequences of confessions or other statements. Miranda rights continue to evolve, but there is no question that this case was a landmark in American jurisprudence.[2]

Another example comes from academia. Early in her work, the psychologist Carol Gilligan realized that researchers in children's moral development, which had previously studied only boys, were downgrading girls' approaches to moral dilemmas because the girls tended to question the dilemmas themselves, rather than judge them in the simple forms presented. The girls would look for cooperative approaches or ask questions to think more expansively about options, rather than just make a legalistic judgment of the stark dilemma as it stood.

This wasn't the kind of answer the researchers were looking for. When the girls saw that—the questioner did not try to hide it—they became confused and uncertain. The questioning sometimes devolved into a kind of browbeating. But wait, Gilligan said. What justified treating the girls' questioning as *lesser*—as morally less developed, or somehow misunderstanding the problem—rather than *different*? Possibly it is even *more* appropriate to question the dilemmas themselves! The girls themselves had no power to make their questions be heard or be taken seriously, but as a Harvard PhD and tenured professor, though also young and female, Gilligan could stand up for them—and did. The effect was to revolutionize moral psychology and modern ethics as well.[3]

---

2. For the full story, read Gary Stuart, *Miranda: The Story of America's Right to Remain Silent* (Tucson: University of Arizona Press, 2008).

3. Gilligan's breakthrough book was *In a Different Voice* (Cambridge, MA: Harvard University Press, 1982). It has inspired many and also provoked a wealth of criticism, revision, and follow-on studies since then.

FOR PRACTICE

6A

Are the questions below questionable? If so, what makes them questionable?

SAMPLE

Question: What is the most important lesson you have learned in your life?

Sample answer:
This is not a bad question, but if I were to have an objection to it, it's that it suggests that you always ought to be learning lessons from your life, which is maybe a bit too moralistic a way to think about living. Maybe I shouldn't necessarily have to mine my own life for "lessons". . . Live and let live, eh?

Comment:
Good point. This answer could go on to ask if there is any better way to put such a question—for example by a grandchild to a grandparent. Maybe *What were some of the best experiences in your life? What were the hardest? Are there things you'd do differently if you could do them over?* It's useful to reflect on life lessons sometimes, but even these questions could also be subtly distancing sometimes. The grandchild could simply ask for advice instead.

---

1. Should people be forced to eat healthier since they won't do it on their own?

2. Are you ever afraid of people knowing who you really are?

3. How do you find time to have young kids and be a professional at the same time?

4. Is this world a divine creation, or merely the product of meaningless collisions of billions of atoms over billions of years?

5.   Shouldn't we spend less money on the military and more on education?

6.   Where are you from? (asked of someone with an unusual accent)

7.   Which came first, the chicken or the egg?

8.   Why are the Arabs sitting on all our oil?

9.   What is the biggest risk you've taken just to prove yourself?

10.   Don't you believe in global warming?

11.   Do you believe in God?

12.   Don't you believe in yourself?

6B

Carefully consider each question below. In what context and to whom might they be questionable questions, and in what contexts and to whom might they be helpful or at least neutral?

SAMPLE

Question: What would you do with a million dollars?

Sample strong answer:
This could be a useful question for someone who actually has a million dollars to do something with. For most of us, though, it's just pie in the sky. The question probably encourages rather useless or distracted daydreaming. It would be more useful to think about why so many of us don't have any serious money to do anything with. Even more to the point, why does money so often seem to be the only way of doing things in the first place?

A _way_ better question would be: What can I do _without_ a million dollars?

Comment:
Right on, we say. This is a great example of reversing a questionable question.

1. Is it better to have loved and lost than never to have loved at all?

2. Are you now, or have you ever been, a member of the Communist Party?

3. What do women want?

4. What should we do about undocumented aliens?

5. Don't you think that white people should stop rapping and stealing the musical traditions of black and brown folks?

6. How might teaching and learning change if we stopped teaching inside of classrooms?

7. How often do you run down other people behind their backs?

8. Who do you look to blame when things go wrong?

9. What is a deep, dark secret of yours that you suspect other people actually have too?

10. What's a nice accountant like you doing in a bar like this?

11. Who would Jesus bomb? (from signs at antiwar rallies)

12. If ignorance is bliss, why aren't more people happy? (bumper sticker)

6C

Here are some statements or exchanges that might involve questionable questions or questionable questioning. (Or, maybe not. Which are which?) If you think they are questionable, identify what makes them so. Then figure out the next line—that is, how to respond briefly but constructively using the methods in this chapter. Finally, explain your thinking.

SAMPLE

Exchange:

A: Eating meat is natural! Humans have always done it.

B: I think most earlier peoples probably did eat meat occasionally, but I am sure they did not eat so much meat or so constantly as us. I mean, McDonald's quarter-pounders with fries and a shake aren't exactly the usual ancient meal.

A: So you think a little organic carrot nugget with spring water is somehow more natural?

Sample answer:

B: Nope.

Explanation: A's rhetorical question uses loaded language. It's meant as mockery. It also poses a false dilemma. My suggested strategy is to just baldly refuse the false dilemma. I'd hope that this would have the effect of lobbing the conversational ball back into A's court.

Comment:

Though terse, this is a sharp and useful answer. Presumably A now has to ask B what B actually does think, and listen to the answer, which would definitely be progress. And it might lead to a more useful, more collaborative discussion about diets and change.

---

1.   **R:** Hey neighbor! It's recycling day and everyone's got their recycling bins out. But we never see yours. Don't you want to do your part to save the planet?

2. **P:** Hey neighbor! It's the Fourth of July and everyone's flying the Stars and Stripes. But we never see yours. Don't you love your country?

3. **X:** It looks like you just aren't aware that your cute little purring pussycat there is actually a mass murderer when she gets outside.

    Y: Fluffy!?

    X: Outdoor cats kill four billion birds and twenty billion small mammals every year, according to the US Fish and Wildlife Service. How can you stand for that?

4. **H** is in a wheelchair in a grocery store and looks to you like he is having trouble reaching certain items on a high shelf.

    You: May I help you?

    H: Did I ask for help?

5. You sit down in a bus for a long ride, and before long the clean-cut and eager person in the seat next to you turns to you and asks:

    G: Are you saved?

    You: It's going to be a hell of a long ride.

    G: Since you mentioned Hell, wouldn't an eternity in damnation be a lot longer?

6. **P:** Life is totally pointless.

    W: Why do you say that?

    P: The Sun is going to blow up and take everything that we love with it.

    W: Well, not for a few billion years, as I understand. [Looking up at Sun] It seems pretty friendly right now.

    P: It's not funny! We're all toast in the end. Who cares how long it takes?

6D

Done with 6C? Good—now go back and take it further. Begin by imagining a response to your answer in 6C. It's not likely to lead to immediate agreement, is it? Maybe the other person will become a little more thoughtful and open-minded—or maybe not. (Would you?) They might even come back with (more) loaded questions or power plays. Your job then is to write the next line once again—to respond effectively and constructively all the same—and then, as in 6C, explain your thinking.

SAMPLE

Exchange so far:

A: Eating meat is natural! Humans have always done it.

B: Most earlier people probably did eat meat occasionally, but I am sure they did not eat so much meat or so constantly as us. I mean, McDonald's quarter-pounders with fries and a shake aren't exactly a traditional meal.

A: Oh right, so you think a little organic carrot nugget with spring water is somehow more natural?

B: Nope.

Sample continuation:

A (after a pause): So you admit that people probably always wanted meat, even if they couldn't get much of it?

B: I imagine they did. A completely animal-free diet would be a fairly new thing in human history. I don't really see a problem with that. Do you?

Explanation: I've made A pay a <u>little</u> better attention with the follow-up question. It's less rhetorical and a little more exploratory. B pretty much responds in kind, shifting the discussion away from "natural" to the possibilities for new diets.

Comment:

Overall this is a well-done continuation. It does lead to better questions from A, and possibly a better understanding between A and B. It might even lead to some greater agreement.

B might want to call out A's term "admit" explicitly, though. It's just one word of A's, but quite revealing: it frames the discussion as a win-lose debate. Such overtones can be hard to notice in the heat of an exchange, but actually B did not claim that non-meat diets were "natural," only that our current meat diets are not. So this is not an "admission" but more like a clarification of a view that A does not yet understand. A's word "admit" still seems to suggest that B has an extreme position that somehow is the opposite of A's, whereas B's actual idea seems to be more nuanced and will be interesting to explore further.

7

For Students

All of your questioning skills apply in school. You will want to ask key critical questions of your readings and class materials, for instance, and you certainly can use creative questioning in school too, just as you would when any other problem or issue seems "stuck." If some of your courses are in philosophy (and we certainly recommend that you take at least a few) you can bring your new skills in philosophical questioning to them too.

In addition, though, school calls upon some special ways of thinking through questions. These are our subject in this final chapter.

Two Kinds of Classes

Naturally there are many kinds of classes, and many classes that mix different approaches to questions. Broadly speaking, though, we can distinguish two quite different ways in which a college or advanced high school class might take up questions.

Question-Answering Classes typically focus on questions that mostly have settled answers from the instructor's and the discipline's point of view. The main aim of these classes is to convey those answers to students. Sometimes they may touch on controversies or uncertainties in the discipline too, but for the most part they are about students learning answers, not engaging in their own questioning. Bloch-Schulman once spoke to a mathematician who said that every single question he gave his college students in their first year of coursework was a question with a definitive answer that he knew.

Or again, introductory biology classes typically answer the basic questions like *What is a cell?*—old hat to biologists, but new to students—and offer a great deal of information with apparent certainty. Trigonometry classes introduce calculating methods of great usefulness and power but some difficulty. And of course there is much to learn. Who would have thought there is so much to know about triangles?

Questioning-Centered Classes take up questions in quite another way—not better or worse, but definitely different. These classes take up questions for the sake of the questions themselves, and to help students begin to think through questions for themselves.

That is, questions don't just frame this kind of course's topic. Instead, questioning itself is daily front and center. The main aim is to understand the questions themselves more deeply, and to learn how to think about them more carefully and thoroughly, especially by marshaling reasons and thinking through ideas in order to make considered decisions and then make compelling cases for them.

For example, consider an introductory philosophy class. Such a course *might* be a Question-Answering Class. In that case it might be structured around various famous philosophers' answers to the question of (say) how we should live. That kind of class' relation to questions would therefore be much like the biology or trigonometry classes'. Your task as a student would be to learn a great deal of information: who said what, and when, and what their arguments were.

It is also possible, though—and more likely—that a philosophy class will be very different. Even when such a class basically surveys the views of a range of philosophers, it will very likely expect students to try to work out their own views in dialogue with the philosophers they are reading—whereas "dialogue" of this sort, and forming your own answers, is not something that most introductory biology or trigonometry classes would even consider.

That is, a philosophy class probably will put the questions themselves front and center. The views of historical or other philosophers will be treated as models and encouragements for students' own thinking and questioning, rather than information to be memorized and repeated back on tests. For this kind of class, it doesn't only matter what certain famous philosophers think about the questions at hand. It matters what—and even more importantly, how—*you* think about them.

And of course these kinds of questions are open, deep, and maybe even unanswerable. But that is not bad. Again, the questions themselves are the thing. No wonder this is a Questioning-*Centered* Class. And the professors, though they may have considered these questions for a long time and have opinions (sometimes quite strong opinions) about them too, also know that they do *not* definitively know the answers to these questions. How exciting!

Of course, again, the difference is not absolute and total. Any decent Questioning-Centered Class will still expect you to master *some* information—to understand the questions, to know the relevant facts that give rise to them, to get the existing range of possible answers straight, to learn and be able to clearly articulate others' views on the issue along with their reasoning, and to learn how to advance and defend your own. That can be a lot! Likewise, many Question-Answering Classes will try to make the questions themselves compelling, rather than *simply* answer them, and may look at controversial and unsettled questions in the field along the way.

Still, the typical Question-Answering Class asks questions chiefly to frame its settled answers, and ask students to answer specific application questions assigned to them. The typical Questioning-Centered Class focuses mostly on the questions themselves and students (and faculty) as questioners. And students need to be able to tell the difference.

So How Can You Tell?

Few classes come labeled as one or the other type. Instead, most instructors and even most disciplines take one model or the other for granted. Fair or not, you may have to figure out for yourself—or do some adept questioning to find out—which kind of class you are in. But usually you will have some good clues.

Class level: introductory classes are more likely to be Question-Answering Classes. This is partly because basic knowledge of a field is usually seen as necessary before anyone can question well in it. Even introductory courses in typically questioning-centered fields like literature or current events often start out with basic information. Still, introductory courses in questioning-centered subjects typically will give students more of a taste of questioning than introductory courses in typically knowledge-focused subjects.

Teaching method: when conveying answers is the main goal, many instructors choose what seems to them to be a straightforward way to do so: lectures, typically based on a textbook and often including PowerPoint or other information-sharing technologies. In this way, settled knowledge is supposed to be most efficiently and reliably communicated.[1]

By contrast, a Questioning-Centered Class naturally will involve, well, a lot of questioning. Likely it will feature more class discussion, possibly debate or other forms of systematic argument, exploring different views without final or authoritative declarations by the teacher. Readings will likely offer differing points of view in diverse voices. Again, questioning itself, in this specific subject, is the main theme of the class, and questioning well is one of the main skills it aims to teach.

Tests: Question-Answering Classes will likely test you on the course content, most likely with true/false, multiple-choice, or short essay tests, or specific problems to which you must apply the methods you have been learning and which have definite right answers. Your job is to get up to speed on this information and on these skills. Typically there is a lot to memorize (do so early and often!—studies show that you will remember best without any cramming) and memorization plays a central role in success.

Questioning-Centered Classes, by contrast, will probably ask you for more extended written work, such as papers and essay examinations in which you need to both show your knowledge of the range of existing views—that is, to show that you understand how others have answered the question and why—and also to capably articulate and defend a view of your own in relation to these other views.

Ask! Finally, if you are still unsure, just ask your professor what kind of class you are getting yourself into. Don't be shy—there is no reason you should necessarily know. Classes may vary a great deal even within the same subject, level, and title. One class called "Introduction to Rap" may be all about the history of rap and variety of rappers. All factual—a standard Question-Answering Class. Another with exactly the same title, and maybe even similar readings and listening material, may be mostly about doing your own rapping. You want to know right away!

---

1. The actual effectiveness of lecturing (or PowerPoint) is not a question for this book, but we certainly encourage you to be curious about how you are schooled and to what extent specific teaching methods work (and for what). After all, you (yeah, *you*!) have a lot at stake in the answers.

Behind the Distinction

One basic assumption of a Questioning-Centered Class is that learning to intelligently answer questions for yourself, and articulate and defend those answers to others, is a valuable skill in itself. After all, one main reason you go to college is to learn how to *think*. Thinking for yourself is essential to taking a responsible part in democratic debate and decision making. It may also be essential to many careers, from the arts to the law.

Yet some types of questions have much more settled answers than others. The quadratic equation, the periodic table, and the time-table of Civil War battles are not really debatable issues. Virtually all the experts agree. Interpretations of *Hamlet*, on the other hand, or whether or when it is ethical to lie in service of supposedly more important values, genuinely do have worthwhile alternative answers. Even the most knowledgeable experts disagree. Therefore, a different way of studying these questions makes sense.

Note also that questions can be settled or unsettled in various ways. Take the question *How could the same man who insisted that "all men are created equal" still have slaves?* In other words, *What was Thomas Jefferson thinking?* Probably there is an answer—it's a psychological question, in part, not just a rhetorical one—but we are unlikely to be able to find it. It is even possible that Jefferson himself did not really know. The question is worth considering anyway, partly because it can prompt parallel questions of ourselves. *If Jefferson could have such a huge blind spot (if that's what it was), what might we be missing?* Naturally, this invites a questioning-centered approach.

Finally, questions may be considered settled in some contexts but unsettled in others. In seminary, for instance, the existence of God is not a real question (though different arguments for and against may well be studied), whereas in most philosophy or religious studies classes in non-religious institutions, it is. Or again, in almost any serious biology class, evolution is taken as a given. Evolution is foundational to the whole discipline. You may be able to take a class on the debate over evolution, but it is unlikely to be in biology proper but possibly in a general studies or contemporary debates class.

Thinking Through Questions in Question-Answering Classes

In classes where the answers are taken as settled, it might seem that there is not much place for thinking through questions. Actually, though, thinking through questions remains essential, but in certain distinctive ways.

Orienting in Class

First of all, you need to know what questions your Question-Answering Class is specifically trying to answer. Your subject may be tapestry, but is your course asking about the mechanics or materials of the weaving, the anthropology of the weavers, or maybe the artistic or historical quality of the product? Or suppose your subject is the Declaration of Independence. Is the course asking about the men who wrote it (Jefferson again, eh?) and their debates, or, say, how the project of American independence was influenced by the Native American nations at the time? Or the actual history of the Declaration's development?

Even courses with the same title can set out to answer very different questions, and you may be thoroughly confused if you imagine you are answering one question when you are really in a class devoted to answering a different one. Or, to put it more positively: you'll be solidly grounded if you are clear what specific questions your course and your professor are aiming to answer for you. Check out the syllabus. Pay close attention to the kinds and types of assessments and assignments: they will tell you a lot about how question-oriented your class is and what the questions are at the heart of it.

You can and sometimes must also ask the same kinds of questions on the level of one day's class, or the readings for it, again at least of yourself and maybe out loud in class as well. Ask *Why are we reading this article? What is it helping us answer? And why are we reading it now?* Don't forget to thank your professors for the answers. Hopefully they'll thank you for the questions!

Clarifying Questions

Good questions in Question-Answering Classes normally focus on gaining and applying information. No surprise: in a good course, the material will be new and should be difficult (but not impossible, of course). Naturally, questions will be needed to clarify the answers too. If something is not clear to you, it's a safe assumption that it is also not clear to at least some other students. So you do them a favor, as well as yourself, by asking.[2]

Active Listening

A lecture is not entertainment. It is also, usually, not meant as a pure information-dump, which after all could be much more efficiently achieved by a reading or even by some kind of app for your phone. Don't turn off your brain! You can think through questions even as you listen.

Even if your response is not invited, your professor's aim is to reenact an intellectual process that you can and should join in. There's drama in it. Right in front of you—OK, at least on a good day—your professor is working through a series of questions and answers that you can enter and share, with your teacher as your energetic guide. And this happens constantly. How lucky can you get?

So go along with her. Try to match intellectual strides—the reasoning and the questioning that prompts each new step—as well as you can. In this way even a Question-Answering Class can teach you not only certain specific answers but also how to think through questions in the field.

It may surprise you to hear that professors sometimes even lecture to each other, for example when we present our work at professional conferences. However, there is always a question-and-answer period afterward, so as we are listening to a presentation/lecture, we are also preparing questions to ask the presenter and for ourselves to consider later. We might want to know about some of the assumptions taken for granted in the work. We might want to know how far the evidence supports the conclusions suggested. Or we might want to know about implications of the work. We'll be thinking carefully (OK, on a good day!) about how the new information or ideas support or challenge our own views.

---

2. And consider this: your professor actually might not know that, or exactly how, the material is hard for you. Once someone really knows a subject or skill, it is easy to forget that and in what way it was hard in the first place. Your faculty are experts, but for that very reason are likely to have this problem. So, asking questions can help them teach better too.

Of course this can *look* like passive listening. But we aren't just sitting there! As we listen, we are *actively* considering and—even if silently—actively asking questions and preparing to ask some out loud. "Active listening" is not an oxymoron: it is a real thing, and moreover it can be your (very interesting and useful) friend.

Asking Good Research Questions

Some Question-Answering Classes require research papers. Likely this will require library work or web-searching. The aim is partly to teach you how to find answers in the field for yourself, as well as to prompt some in-depth learning in some aspect of the field that especially interests you.

Research questions may be assigned to you. If so, appreciate them, and study them carefully. Your professor is aiming to teach you by example about good research questions in the field, as well as to give your research a strong head start.

If you must pose your research questions yourself, start with background reading, and/or think about questions that have already arisen for you. Aim to frame an actual question. Don't say, "I am researching universal languages," for instance, or even something as specific as "Esperanto." These are still just *topics*. What is your *question?*

Make your question specific, not too vague or broad (though also not too narrow). Reading about universal languages, a natural question might be *What is the best universal language?* However, answering this question would require a survey of all of the main contenders—there are at least three or four—and also might be rather opinionated for research proper. More useful and specific might be questions like *What are the acknowledged strong points of each of the current most popular universal languages?* or *How readily learnable are they?* This way, specific data come into play. To explore the second question you could even take some initiative and try to learn a universal language yourself.

As you tailor your research question, be sure you have the time and resources to answer it. Can you find out the relevant information and write it up in time and at the depth your question requires? Or, if you are doing an empirical study, are you trained in the appropriate methods? If you need subjects, lab equipment, or space, can you get them?

Finally, be sure to make your question *interesting*. Why work on a question that no one, including you, really cares about? Working on a question that matters, and matters to you, will probably not make it easier, but your heart will certainly be in it. And you may end by making a real contribution.

Questioning Questions in Question-Answering Classes

Question-Answering Classes, intentionally or not, tend to discourage questions that challenge key assumptions in the discipline. Some teachers may not have considered such questions at all and find them irrelevant or unsettling. Many will not welcome them from students, especially students who they think do not understand the field well enough to question it in this way. And, often, fair enough. In many fields and in many classes, again, you really do first need to master the non-controversial information before knowing enough to ask fundamental questions of the field.

On the other hand, even a field's most basic questions *can* be questioned, and sometimes young outsiders are the best ones to do so. Even whole disciplines can be built on assumptions that turn out to be, well . . . questionable.

Until recently, for example, the main questions in clinical psychology were about how to help those who were in need of help: for example, depressed, anxious, or having a hard time in life. Recently, a new set of questions have emerged, often referred to as "positive psychology," which ask about people who are doing and feeling well, and trying to help them fully flourish. Yet for a long time a student who saw psychology in a more positive way might well have been discouraged from questioning the reigning ideas and questions.

There is a place for fundamental questioning, then, even in Question-Answering classes. If you are so inclined, keep alert for good occasions, have your questions well-prepared, and enter the discussion in an open-minded and constructive way. There may after all be good answers. And remember, once again, that good questioning does sometimes take courage.

Thinking Through Questions in Questioning-Centered Classes

A Questioning-Centered Class likely calls for wider participation than a lecture, with multiple points of view being voiced and without the authority of more or less settled answers. This kind of class requires your own questioning. If you just sit in such a class and expect definitive answers that you can write down and replicate on a test, you'll miss the most important skill the class is trying to teach. Likely you will not get a very good grade, either.

There is another and opposite pitfall, however, with this kind of class. Since they are not based on settled facts and teacher authority, it may seem that "anything goes." It may seem easy to jump into this sort of class. Everyone's entitled to their opinion, right?

Again, though, not so fast. To just broadcast your opinions, it would be a lot less expensive to go out on the street or (like lots of folks, it seems) to some online forum. But will anyone listen? And why should they? (Do you?) Once again, worthwhile opinions need to be carefully thought through, based on real knowledge, and open to rethinking and even change. Even though they are "opinions," they still take time to develop, and they need to be advanced in dialogue with a variety of views of others already in the conversation. These are the skills of thinking through questions that a Questioning-Centered Class aims to teach.

Unpack the Backstory

As we have been saying, any good Questioning-Centered Class will require that you actually know what you are talking about. In fact, take that as the basic rule: know what you are talking about!

Should white people rap? Interesting question, eh? But what is actually being asked? And why? Don't assume that you know already. An off-the-top-of-your-head opinion, just reacting to the question, is, honestly, pretty useless. Instead, try to get the understanding needed for a well-founded answer. What's the backstory here? Why has the question come up now and in this particular form? Then ask what are the main points of view, and what are the reasons for them. What are the existing arguments?

People in the rap community point to a long history of white musicians popularizing and profiting from musical forms that originated with black artists, all the way back to jazz and the blues.

"Cultural appropriation" is one term for it. Surely it is time, they argue, to break that pattern. Couldn't—shouldn't—it be different with rap?

Exploring, you may ask: *Has* rap to date really been basically a black (or black and brown) art form? Arguably yes, though we'll need to leave the investigation to you. On the other hand, have there been influential white rappers too? (Also yes . . . it gets complicated.) And haven't many of those influential white rappers been brought into the rap scene by more famous black artists (both the respected, like Eminem, who was a protégé of Dr. Dre, and the less respected, like Iggy Azalea, who was the protégé of T.I.)? (More complicated, still.)

Since it is key to the issue, you'll also need to explore how far the pattern of cultural appropriation actually holds. You'll quickly come, as well, to a spirited debate over whether there were realistic alternatives to it. We certainly do not want to repeat old patterns of injustice. Then again, can a culture rightly be said to somehow have sole rights to an art form? Maybe art is more like, say, a gift—a point made beautifully about a white musician by Dizzy Gillespie's famous line "You can't steal a gift."

Again, you see that there is much to unpack and think about here. And you can see that *now*—but only now—you may become able to thoughtfully enter the discussion yourself.

Taking a Stand

You can learn a question's backstory and uncover the facts and existing perspectives on it without necessarily taking a position on it. Sometimes you might even resolve to take part in a discussion without inserting your own opinion into it at all. Or maybe, even after thoroughly unpacking a question, you still genuinely don't know what to think—often a very reasonable response. Get good at this, and you might even find yourself a useful career as a mediator or facilitator, places where objectively minded people can be a big help.

Still, we often want or need to put forward answers of our own—to join the conversation or debate with our own voices. Maybe you are in a Questioning-Centered Class that requires you to do so. Thus, based on what you and/or your classmates have found so far, you can now try to decide what you actually think, at this point anyway, and to spell out your reasons carefully and logically, so that you can then test your answers against the views of others, answering their questions in turn, as well as posing more pointed questions to them, and hopefully working out still better views together.

In any case, the key lesson of a Questioning-Centered Class is that taking a stand is not the *first* step, but well into the process of thinking through questions. It is not the last step, either, though, because you may learn as much, and change your views several times again, once you and your classmates can carefully consider and—yes—question the stand you first take.

At some point, finally, you will find yourself needing your questioning and thinking skills beyond a classroom, and probably where the stakes are more serious as well: in some other subject, in your career or family, in public life or in moments of social or political crisis. Not just a class but life itself sometimes requires us to be questioning-centered. Your class, and this book, have finished their work when you find that thinking through questions in this way too has become something you look forward to and even find yourself doing almost automatically. Look forward to that—and use your new skills well.

Humility

Many questions that are typically the focus of Questioning-Centered Classes have been debated, endlessly, for good reason. They are really hard to answer! Exceptionally smart, careful, clear, and thoughtful people disagree about them. In fact, it may well be that some of the smartest people who have ever lived disagree about them—this is why they are especially good topics for Questioning-Centered Classes in the first place.

So approach them with humility, modesty, and curiosity. Don't take the question as an opportunity to deliver your opinion as if it were a fact. Things that seem obvious to you at first might well—in the light of good conversation and engagement—seem a lot less obvious, or not even true in the end. Anyway, no one is much interested in more loud but uninformed opinions.

Of course you should still get in the mix, discuss and offer your thoughts. That's how you learn—if you are open to the learning. Shockingly enough, it's always possible that you are wrong—or, at least, not completely right. Try to allow—even, help—a better opinion to emerge and develop, rather than just assert what you already believe. A little humility can go a long way.

FOR PRACTICE

7A

Considering what you currently know about the following questions, would you classify the most likely class on each subject as mainly Question-Answering or Questioning-Centered? Why?

SAMPLE

Topic: Is Pluto a planet?

Sample answer:
This topic would come up in astronomy classes, which are in the natural sciences and typically Question-Answering Classes. With a little research I have learned that a number of Pluto-like bodies have recently been detected in the outer solar system, which are more like moons than the massive gas planets that end with Uranus. Pluto has come to look like just another random lost moon. This is why the question of how to classify Pluto is controversial among astronomers (Robert Roy Britt, "Pluto Demoted," Space.com, August 24, 2006, https://www.space.com/2791-pluto-demoted-longer-planet-highly-controversial-definition.html, accessed August 29, 2019). Either we have to say that there are a lot more "planets" in the solar system than we thought, or we'd better just stop with Uranus. It's a questioning-centered topic since astronomers are still questioning about it.

Comment:
We appreciate the research here, as always. And the points about Pluto are key parts of the background information needed to enter into the debate. Still, budding natural scientists might find it surprising, and helpful, to learn that questioning-centered topics may turn up even in science classes.

---

1. So *is* it problematic for white people to rap?

2. Are humans inherently a destructive species?

3.   How might world history have been different if the great
       fifteenth- and sixteenth-century voyages of exploration
       had been Chinese?

4.   What is an ecosystem and how does it function?

5.   What is the best way to protect the Everglades?

6.   Does God exist?

7.   Could computers have minds?

8.   What, if anything, cannot be forgiven?

9.   What is the nature of evil?

10.   What is the most effective diet for losing weight?

11.   Why does anyone find the Kardashians the slightest bit
       interesting in any way whatsoever?

12.   How likely is Earth to be visited by space aliens?

7B

Suppose you are a teacher designing a class session addressing each
of the questions in 7A. How might you help students think through
each question, and why?

SAMPLE

Topic: Is Pluto a planet?

Sample strong answer:

Since astronomers themselves debate this question, students
might reenact the debate in a Questioning-Centered Class session.
This would require them to study and understand the different
positions, and well enough not just to repeat the basic ideas but

to defend and develop them in debate. The instructor could coach them on how to listen and to argue scientifically. In this way I'd hope they would also come to realize that each point of view makes sense, and perhaps that the choice might plausibly go either way. They could even hold their own vote in the end.

Comment:

This is a nice way of considering how students might engage in the discussion and debate. They might also more concretely recognize science as an open-ended human endeavor.

7C

Below are some topics or draft questions. Are they good research questions as they stand? How might you improve those that aren't?

SAMPLE

Topic: Lie detectors

Sample strong answer:

First off, this is not a question, just a broad subject. What is the question?

It's tempting to ask: Do lie detectors really work? However, lie detectors have been studied to death. I mean, there is a great deal of controversy on the subject and many studies on both sides, and it doesn't seem like another broad survey of the debate would be too helpful, except maybe for background.

Some more useful or informative specific research questions might be:

- Why are lie detector results usually not admissible in courts of law?

- Are there specific circumstances under which lie detector tests are recognized to be valid?

- Are there alternative and more accurate ways to determine if someone is lying?

Comment:
Good questions. Note that a good move with the last one might be to add an expansive question: If there are no good alternatives at present, what would it take to invent one?

For another approach, you could also take a lie detector test yourself and carefully reflect on the experience. There is an interesting but not well-known body of research using this first-person approach. Here you might make an unusual and helpful contribution.

1.   What is the best form of exercise?

2.   Does raising the minimum wage overburden employers?

3.   Fracking

4.   What is the exact best dosage of vitamin C to prevent colds?

5.   Gender verification in sports

6.   How much inflation is too much?

7.   Did Antonio Salieri really poison Mozart?

8.   9/11 conspiracy theories

9.   Do a significant number of autistic children live in my neighborhood?

10. Is DNA-based ancestry testing valid?

11. Are Republicans more likely than Democrats to be racist?

12. Sex

For Further Practice

We conclude with some sets of questions to which you are invited to bring all of your questioning skills. Our only instruction is this: give them some time.

A

Here is a varied set of simple questions to encounter "cold"—not framed by any chapter's topic. Take them as you see fit, and consider how you might answer or go on constructively in some other way.

1. Parrot to passer-by in pet shop: "Can't you talk?"[1]

2. One student to another in a café: "Do I think too much?"

3. What's the you-est thing about you?

4. What part of *No* don't you understand?

5. If you could find out the for-sure answer to any one question, right now, what would it be?

6. What do you do when an endangered species of animal is eating an endangered species of plant?

7. Should we clone humans?

8. Is a hot dog a sandwich?

9. How could this class be less exciting?

10. Why *did* the chicken cross the road?

11. Fries with that?

12. How many angels can dance on the head of a pin?

---

1. Reader's Digest, https://www.rd.com/jokes/funny-stories/.

B

We asked some of our students for their favorite questions, or questions they often hear their peers asking. Here is a sampling of their responses. We encourage you to appreciate and reflect on these—and think of your own.

1. Who can you really trust and why?

2. What is the best feeling in the world?

3. Is it all just in your head?

4. What is your spirit animal?

5. What could replace money as an economic system?

6. Can you really get rid of stigma, or does it just change form?

7. Is there a most important material possession?

8. Can you unlearn something?

9. How many random people's photos am I in?

10. Which is worse, failing or never trying?

11. Why do I matter?

12. What significance do last words have?

C

Here are some more detailed questions for your provocation and enjoyment.

1. If someone told you that she always lies, should you (*could* you?) believe her?

2.   As far as we know at first glance, a website that calls itself a "fact checker" is only another website, right? Just because they call themselves a fact checker, though, does not mean that actual, objective fact-checking is actually their agenda. How can we tell? How do we fact-check the fact checkers?

3.   Genetic testing has allowed us to answer questions we couldn't have imagined seriously investigating before. Today some people are discovering that their biological parents or relatives are not who they always thought they were. It's fascinating, though they are not always glad they asked. Can you think of other kinds of questions, unanswerable or maybe even unaskable now, that we might be able to answer in the future—for better or worse?

4.   Should geologists distinguish a new geological epoch, starting in very recent times and named after human beings, considering humanity's massive impact on the planet? (Look up the debate over the "Anthropocene.")

5.   *Why didn't the Jews resist the Holocaust?* Historian Berel Lang calls this an especially "mischievous" question. Consider Lang's argument at https://collections.ushmm.org /search/catalog/bib89300 and expand on your and his answers.

6.   In a debate during the 1988 presidential election between George H. W. Bush and Michael Dukakis, the first question of the debate, posed to Dukakis, was this: *If your wife were raped and murdered, would you favor an irrevocable death penalty for the killer?* Dukakis answered no, and went on to explain his opposition to the death penalty—a reasonable enough answer, but he was widely criticized for not showing enough passion or "strength." Writing up alternative answers was even a small cottage industry among commentators after the debate. Dukakis went on to lose the election, and many saw this moment as the beginning of his decline in the polls. Think about how you would answer such a question if you had been Dukakis.

7.   Only three countries in the world have not adopted the metric system (kilometers, milligrams . . .) for measurements: Liberia, Myanmar, and the United States of America. Is this a problem? If so, what could be done about it?

8.   Too many of the current forms of political protest are so obviously pushed into invisibility or irrelevance that the protestors become embittered and cynical—or turn to violence. What would be three more productive forms of protest?

9.   Try designing a society without knowing what your own status will be within it. If you don't know whether you'll be a janitor or a CEO, a movie star or a felon (or both), how will you distribute your society's rights and powers? Why?

10.   Winston Churchill once memorably said that "democracy is the worst possible form of government, except for all the others." Can you work out any better ones? Like what?

11.   As retribution for the most serious of crimes we tend to think of only the death penalty or life imprisonment. What other options might there be? How else might we approach the whole question of punishment and prison?

12.   Pick a conspiracy theory: that UFOs are alien spacecraft and the government knows all about it; that the CIA killed JFK; that the 9/11 attacks were an inside job; or for that matter even the accusation that global climate change is a made-up fear to help bring down capitalism. Consider this theory as a mode of questioning the official explanation of those events. When and where do you think this mode of questioning is questionable? When and where is it not?

For Teachers

This appendix outlines some of your co-authors' methods for teaching effectively with this book. You will teach with it in your own ways, of course, and we look forward to hearing from teachers as well as students about how it works out for you. Email us directly (sschulman@elon.edu, weston@elon.edu) or in care of Hackett Publishing Company via www.hackettpublishing.com/thinking-through -questions-support.

As we say in the Introduction, *Thinking Through Questions* is meant to offer more inviting and wider-lens introductions to some key kinds of questioning than are usually offered to students today. Especially in critical thinking courses and textbooks, it is common to just launch into tools for critical questioning without explaining why they are so necessary, or how critical thinking relates to other kinds of questioning that may call for quite different and sometimes opposite methods. Sometimes critical thinking is even treated like the only kind of thinking there is—certainly the only kind of questioning we need to train.

This book paints a broader picture of critical questioning's place among other key modes of questioning, and grounds it more explicitly in some very basic epistemology. Chapter 1 outlines reasons why questioning as such is so necessary, and Chapters 3, 4, and 5 explain why quite different forms of questioning are necessary for different purposes. Free association, as just one example, is definitely *not* helpful in critical questioning, but it is essential to expansive questioning. Students should know how and why. The same for philosophical questioning. The same for learning to recognize and effectively respond to questionable questions.

We therefore invite teachers to consider assigning this book early on in your courses, and/or right alongside the other kinds of questioning your courses mainly address. If you ask students to read the whole book as a way of introducing and framing the class, they should be able to work it through in a week or two, especially if you use the exercises sparingly. In that case we also recommend returning to this book throughout your class, highlighting its applicability when and where appropriate. Or, you might pair parts of this book with more traditional material to call forth (or call into question) the questions that are already part of the class content. We've tried to offer a supple text and ample exercises to support both kinds of uses.

Here are some specific suggestions chapter by chapter.

Chapters 1 and 2: You might consider offering a whole course about questions, broadly considered—maybe call it "The Philosophy of Questions" or "Philosophy and Inquiry." Read biographies of great questioners or great moments of questioning. Explore various kinds of questioning, ideally quite different from each other. Watch good attorneys conduct cross-examinations, talk to chemists and marketers and psychotherapists and children's book writers. Go more deeply into the kinds of questioning detailed in this book: there are many good books on each.

We ask students to do a lot of practice. They enjoy this kind of work; it gives practical results that can make a real difference; and anyway, in the end, in our view, there is just no other way to develop the skills. Learning to think through questions is much more like learning to play jazz piano, say, than learning music theory. Reading or lecturing about it can only be prelude. Students need practice both to hone their skills and their timing, learning when to use which technique for greatest effect.

Classes can often be workshops and discussions based on the exercises. Among other things, have the students sometimes work through sample questions in small groups and then present their results to the class. Organize forums, panel discussions, or courtroom-like scenarios to vary the settings and increase engagement and challenge.[1]

In the **For Practice** exercises we've tried to offer a wide range of challenges and pick an interesting and varied range of topics. Of course you can also supplement with your own. Even better, or in addition, ask students to generate their own lists of questions, maybe before doing any reading at all. (See also "For Further Practice" question set B). A useful book to orient both you and your students to thinking through questions beyond the usual academic frame is Inge Bell and Bernard McGrane's *This Book Is Not Required* (SAGE Publications, many editions)

There is no necessary order to the chapters after Chapter 2. You can read them in any sequence that suits your class, or focus only

---

1. Stephen highly recommends Anthony's book *Teaching as the Art of Staging* (Sterling, VA: Stylus, 2019) for working out this kind of pedagogy. (Thanks, pal.—AW)

on some, leaving the others for background reading. This should allow you to pair this book's chapters with specific course themes and content.

Chapter 3: Many full-scale textbooks are available for critical thinking classes, including one by David Morrow and Anthony Weston, *A Workbook for Arguments* (third edition, Hackett Publishing, 2020), companion to Weston's little guidebook, *A Rulebook for Arguments* (fifth edition, Hackett Publishing, 2017). But few of these, as we have been saying, begin by giving critical questioning a broad context and an approachable, motivating general rationale. *Thinking Through Questions* is meant to do just that.

As far as pedagogy for this chapter specifically, consider mounting some in-class scenarios that require critical questioning, such as mock presidential debates or courtroom trials. More involved scenarios could complement these with slower-motion but deeper questioning, such as setting up student teams to peer-review each other's papers or review other teams' inferences from small data sets on some new subject that you prepare and hand out. Or, practice telling "fake news" from real news. Bring in a variety of newspapers or explore a variety of online news sources and compare and contrast them. Ask your librarian for a current list of websites designed to help students distinguish well-grounded web information from manipulative or comic sites. (Here are two classics to get you started: https://www.dhmo.org/facts.html and https://www.ovaprima.org/.)

Chapter 4: Expansive or creative questioning is a much less commonly taught subject than critical questioning, but arguably is just as essential. To be able to see the world in the light of possibility is a vital thinking skill as well. We believe it is one of the most vital of all.

A wide range of books on creative thinking are available today. Some focus solely on methods. Most are not textbooks per se, but are narratives by product designers, artists, social change activists, "imagineers." All to the good, we say. These are the frontline expansive questioners, and often they do the types of work that our students may someday take up.

Pedagogically the key word again is *practice*. Practicing creative thinking can be a thoroughly engaging activity in a classroom. This chapter's box on "Inviting Novel Associations" may give you a bit of a feeling for it. Put students in brainstorming groups, or remix the groups if they're already working together.

If you are not used to this kind of questioning yourself, the key practice for you as the teacher is *patience*. Expansive thinking is not so familiar, and can readily be undercut from the teacher's side as well. Try to give the methods enough time to work, especially the more improbable or uncomfortable methods like novel association, if you are used to more analytical thinking. Resist moving too fast to edit or tone down students' initial ideas, once they come up with them, or hanging on to "given" problems rather than rethinking them in turn (e.g., suppose we don't need *better* cars but, in the end, *no* cars). Work to wholeheartedly model a thoroughly open-ended approach. Give students a lot of space and also a lot of provocation—for they too, more often than you might think, really need to be nudged into using some of these methods. Don't let them stop with ideas that are only a little outside of the box. Keep "plussing" instead. Err on the side of asking too much, not expecting just "good enough."

Chapter 5: Consider using this chapter as the very first short reading in a philosophy course, especially if it is a thoroughly Questioning-Centered Class (use Chapter 7 too, then). Starting from the philosophical presuppositions of everyday beliefs and actions is a vivid way of making the point that philosophy can be a thoroughly practical business. Can you help the more esoteric themes and forms of "extreme questioning" emerge from these? Consider following up with narratives of real philosophers at work: on hospital ethics committees, Truth and Reconciliation Commissions, dialoguing with artificial intelligences and other science-fictional possibilities . . . you name it. A whole course, or a major chunk of a course, could even explore hypothetical questions (thought-experiments)—for moral consistency and much more.

Chapter 6: One engaging method is to set up a contest for the most questionable questions. Several contests, in fact. One could be for "found" questions—from the media, personal conversations or debates, or from reading. Another could invite invented ones. Divide the class in half and have each group come up with the most questionable questions they can. Intersperse these with a few perfectly innocent questions and then bring them back to the other group, who can practice both detecting the questionable ones and responding effectively. Do this in real-time conversations but also in writing, so that students can practice slower reflectiveness too.

Chapter 7: If your class is a general introduction to college thinking, you might start with this chapter: that is, with the basic distinction between Question-Answering Classes and Questioning-Centered Classes. Ask your students: *Which type is this very class? How do you know? And what follows?* Send them out then to ask the same question about their other classes, and bring back and compare their answers.

Touching on this theme early on can also be useful for philosophy classes generally. Students coming from the sciences, especially, or from rather rote high school classes, are often confused by the quite different goals in philosophy and other college-level humanities classes. Chapter 7 should help them get oriented in Questioning-Centered Classes and, in particular, in philosophy classes, while hopefully deepening their understanding of and engagement in Question-Answering Classes generally as well.

Finally, the heartiest best wishes! We hope that this book can contribute in some small way both to more effective classes and to your own enjoyment of thinking through questions in all aspects of life.

About the Authors

Your co-authors are long-time colleagues in the Philosophy Department at Elon University in North Carolina. We are also both thoroughgoing questioners. As such, both of us have found, over the years, that friends and others are sometimes surprised by certain moves we make when questions come up. They're even occasionally impressed. We seem to have something to offer when the matter of questioning is involved.

Bloch-Schulman was the inaugural winner (2017) of the Prize for Excellence in Teaching Philosophy, awarded by the American Philosophical Association, the American Association of Philosophy Teachers, and the Teaching Philosophy Association. He has been researching teaching and learning, and teaching faculty about teaching philosophy, for many years. As part of his research, he conducts "think-alouds" with everyone from high school students through college professors. He has found that certain people think through questions in a distinctively open-ended and persistently self-possessed way. Philosophers, especially, may decline to answer questions as asked. Instead, they may say that it is not a good question; they may ask a different question and address it instead; they may even reject the question entirely. They approach questions not as fixed or "given"—that is, not as just needing answers exactly as posed—but rather as open and fluid, calling for reframing, un-framing, and occasionally for rejection.

We think Bloch-Schulman's experiment illustrates something very important that philosophers know, have been trained to do, and have as a habit of mind: namely, once again, that questions are powerful but always, well, open to question. Still, as important as questioning questions is for how philosophers think, as far as we know it is not typically a focus of how philosophers teach their own students. While they may ask students to learn what questions motivated famous philosophers, they typically don't focus on how students themselves can learn to be better at thinking through questions. We'd like to change that. This is one of the key skills we have tried to distill in this book.

Bloch-Schulman tends to question by focusing on the unstated assumptions that frame and shape the typical questions (and answers!) we think are important. For example, in a recent class about the so-called Kaepernick kneeling controversy, students expected to focus on the question: *Did he do the right thing by kneeling?* Instead, Bloch-Schulman asked students to examine the national anthem and its history, the invention of racism and the impact of racism on America, the agreement between the military and the NFL that drives the displays of patriotism at the start of most sports events, the history of protest in sports, and the role of other athletes (in particular, the women of the WNBA) as predecessors to Kaepernick's protest. The class ended up not asking *Did Kaepernick do the right thing by protesting by taking a knee?* but rather *What is the most controversial aspect of what happened?* That is, they examined the way the controversy is framed to question whether the question *Did he do the right thing?* is even the right question.

Weston is the author of the most widely used short primer in critical thinking today, *A Rulebook for Arguments* (Hackett Publishing), now in its fifth edition (2017) and accompanied by a full-scale textbook, *A Workbook for Arguments,* co-authored with David Morrow (third edition, 2019). He has also penned a number of other books, most of which are broadly about better questions, from *How to Re-Imagine the World* (New Society Publishers, 2007), addressing imagination generally, to an early book about ethics called *Toward Better Problems* (Temple University Press, 1992)—which might just as well have been called *Toward Better Questions.* At Elon, he has been honored as both Teacher of the Year (2002) and Scholar of the Year (2007).

Since *Rulebook* is his best-known book, people tend to be surprised when Weston insists that the familiar argumentative and analytical skills are not the only or even necessarily the most important questioning skills we can develop. Often at least as essential, he argues, is the ability to strategically reframe questions so that expansive and constructive responses are invited. Imagination is another key skill, both for head and heart; it comes in when we ask how *else* might we deal with the problem or issue before us, besides the standard answers to it, which sometimes even become part of the problem themselves.

For Weston, then, even critical questioning is often very specifically expansive in addition, and underneath. Indeed, one of his favorite questions is *What would be a better alternative?* His way of thinking critically about today's education is to try to work out better ways to teach and better ways to build classrooms or other learning spaces. His way of thinking critically about today's ways of living is to work out better ones—which is why, for one thing, he is now heavily involved in building Hart's Mill Ecovillage, an alternative intentional community in central North Carolina. Related, Weston's other favorite question is *What's the next step?* or *How could we go further?* "Plussing" need not be a one-time thing! If perhaps you were a little surprised, and then maybe intrigued, by exercise 4C, you get the picture.

In general, as we hope you have seen many times over in this book, we believe that questioning can be a far more intriguing and inventive process than people are often taught to think. And it's essential, even when it is not so easy or enjoyable. We hope this book inspires and guides you to question mindfully, question regularly (though not all the time), and question well.

Visual Thinking Space

Visual Thinking Space

Visual Thinking Space